ANIMAL RIGHTS: THE ABOLITIONIST APPROACH

Gary L. Francione
Anna Charlton

EXEMPLA PRESS

For the abolitionist vegans throughout the world who are dedicated to building a grassroots movement that seeks to shift the paradigm from animals as property to animals as persons.

Contents

Acknowledgements

Thanks to Elizabeth Collins, Mariana C. Gonzalez, Frances McCormack, and Linda McKenzie for editing, and to Mariana C. Gonzalez, Vincent Guihan, and Foppe de Haan for helping in the production process. Mariana C. Gonzalez served as project manager.

We express our deep appreciation to our friend and comrade, Sue Coe, who did the artwork on the cover specifically for this book.

Preface: A Revolution of the Heart

This book is about a revolution—a revolution of the heart.

Throughout the world, women, people of color, children, the elderly, the mentally disabled, the poor, and other humans are treated as second-class citizens by the corporate patriarchy that runs the show. Yet, nonhuman animals are, in many ways, the most vulnerable among us. The exploitation of animals is pervasive, entrenched, and unspeakably horrific. Not only can we torture and kill them with complete impunity; we are expected to do so. We at least pay lip service to the idea that violence against humans is morally problematic, but violence against nonhumans is generally considered to be a virtue, particularly when it is characterized as being "humane." Those who refuse to participate in the carnage are regarded as abnormal and antisocial even by the large animal charities, which claim that we can satisfy our moral obligations to nonhuman animals by exploiting them in a supposedly more "gentle" manner.

It is wrong to characterize those who produce animal products as our "enemies" to let ourselves off the hook. Institutional exploiters are fulfilling a demand—*from us*. They are simply doing what *we* want them to do. They act wrongly in satisfying our demand. But it is *our* demand to which they respond.

We must abolish, and not regulate, animal exploitation. The abolition of animal exploitation requires a paradigm shift. It requires a recognition that violence against the vulnerable is inherently wrong. It calls for a revolution of the heart.

That revolution must occur within each and every one of us. And it can if we want it to. It starts with our own veganism—our not eating, wearing, or otherwise using animals—not as some sort of "flexitarian lifestyle" issue, but as a basic, fundamental, and non-negotiable commitment to nonviolence and justice for nonhuman animals. Veganism, as a moral imperative, represents our recognition that we have no moral justification for using animals—however "humanely"—for our purposes. It continues with our

3

daily efforts to educate others in creative, positive, and nonviolent ways about veganism—something that each of us can do if we want to. Every day, we have opportunities to educate family, friends, colleagues at work, and people whom we encounter in a store or on a bus. Is it easier to write a check to someone else than do the work ourselves? Of course it is. But it won't work.

To achieve justice, we do not need large animal charities. Indeed, the more we rely on them, the further we will stray from our goal. The large animal groups are *businesses*. They sell welfare reform. They sell "happy exploitation" in the form of larger cages for hens, more room for pigs and calves, slaughter processes that are more "humane," and the like. They help people to feel better about continuing to consume animals although many experience nagging feelings of guilt about it. Many love their nonhuman companions and treat them as family members, but stick forks into other animals and, on some level, recognize the moral disconnect. However, the animal charities tell us not to worry—that if we make a donation, they will "minimize" animal suffering and will supposedly eliminate the "worst abuses." Donors, these charities say, can still continue to participate in exploiting animals, comfortable in the knowledge that they as donors have paid to make it all more "humane."

As a result, the term "animal rights" has become used in an opportunistic way that is confused and diluted. We are all "animal rights activists" now, but little has changed for the animals we exploit.

We need to transform the way in which humans think about nonhumans and about nonviolence. We need a grassroots movement that demands justice for animals and promotes the abolition, not the regulation, of animal exploitation. The means that we choose to get to abolition must be consistent with the end. We cannot promote "humane" exploitation as a means to achieve no exploitation. That is both morally and practically unsound. We need a grassroots movement that promotes veganism as a moral imperative.

The Abolitionist Approach to Animal Rights represents a way of thinking about animal ethics that can facilitate the paradigm shift which needs to occur if anything is ever going to change for animals. In this book, we discuss six principles that make up the Abolitionist Approach. We present a blueprint for a grassroots movement that can help us create a vegan world.

At the core of the Abolitionist Approach is the idea that the primary moral issue involves the *use* of animals, and not the *treatment* of animals. Less suffering is, of course, better than more suffering. It is better to beat one's slaves nine times a week rather than ten. But reducing the harm a bit does not address the fundamental injustice of the institution of slavery. Similarly, confining chickens in an "enriched" cage rather than in a conventional cage not only fails to significantly improve the welfare of the chickens, but it also does not address the injustice of treating animals as property—as things that exist only as resources for humans. Indeed, the message that is sent to the public is that it is a morally good thing to eat eggs from chickens confined in "enriched" cages. Moreover, we must make clear that there is no morally coherent distinction between meat and other animal "foods," or between fur and wool, or between dogs, cats, dolphins, whales or nonhuman primates on one hand, and chickens, pigs, cows, fish or rodents on the other.

Those who claim to be "abolitionists" but who promote welfare reform and single-issue campaigns are not "abolitionists" as we use that term in this book. Indeed, their position—that "abolitionists" can promote welfare reform and single-issue campaigns—is the very position that we reject in favor of an abolitionist position that focuses on veganism as a moral imperative: as what anyone who cares morally about animals is obligated to do *today*. So those who promote welfare reform campaigns or single-issue campaigns can call themselves "abolitionists" if they want, but they are not abolitionists as we understand that term. Abolitionists are those who say *today* that animal use is immoral, unjust, and must end, and that each of us can do something *today* to bring about the end of the horrible violence that is animal exploitation. Abolitionists engage in creative, nonviolent vegan education but they are always clear that if animals matter morally, veganism is the only morally acceptable response, and that those who are not vegan are participating directly in animal exploitation.

* * * * * *

The Abolitionist Approach represents a body of work and experience stretching back for three decades. We were both involved in the animal movement in the early 1980s. We both volunteered with a number of animal advocacy groups and we both did a considerable amount of pro bono legal work for these groups and for individual animal advocates. From 1990 to 2000, we ran the Rutgers University School of Law Animal Rights Law Clinic, which was the first entity of its kind anywhere in the world. Students received academic credit for learning about animal rights theory as they worked on real legal cases that involved animal issues. We have both been writing about these issues for decades. From this perspective, we propose a radical change.

This book is intended as an introduction to the Abolitionist Approach. Although it covers all of the main ideas of this approach to animal rights, it cannot possibly cover these ideas completely. So please treat the discussion of each principle as providing a survey of the ideas relevant to that principle. We have provided citation notes where needed and we encourage you to read the cited sources so that you can learn more about the issue or point being discussed. Each discussion is also followed by a section that provides further reading so that you can learn about these ideas on a deeper level.

In the past, we have used the feminine pronoun to avoid reinforcing the sexism reflected in the default use of the male pronoun. In this book, we use the singular "they" when we are referring to humans to reflect current discussions about sex and gender. The final essay, *A Note About the Abolitionist Approach, Morality, Religion, and Spirituality,* was written in 2012 and is being reprinted here. It retains the use of the feminine pronoun.

The Abolitionist Approach to Animal Rights: A Manifesto

Principle One

Abolitionists maintain that all sentient beings, human or nonhuman, have one right—the basic right not to be treated as the property of others.

Summary

Animals are classified as property and are used exclusively as resources for humans. Although we claim to regard animals as having moral value and to not be just things, their status as property means that they have no moral value; they have only economic value. We recognize that treating humans as property is inconsistent with recognizing humans as members of the moral community. We accept as a fundamental moral principle that all humans, irrespective of their particular characteristics, must be accorded the basic moral right not to be property. On this principle rests the universal condemnation of human slavery. The property status of animals means that animals are considered to be things, irrespective of what we say to the contrary. There is no way to distinguish humans from nonhumans that can justify withholding from all sentient nonhumans the same right that we accord to all humans. We need to recognize that all sentient beings are equal for the purpose of not being used exclusively as human resources. The Abolitionist Approach maintains that all animal use—however supposedly "humane"—is morally unjustified.

Principle Two

Abolitionists maintain that our recognition of this one basic right means that we must abolish, and not merely regulate, institutionalized animal exploitation, and that abolitionists should not support welfare reform campaigns or single-issue campaigns.

Summary

Recognizing the right of animals not to be used as property requires that we abolish the institutionalized exploitation of nonhuman animals, and not just regulate it to make it more "humane." Abolitionists reject animal welfare campaigns. They also reject single-issue campaigns, a particular sort of regulatory campaign that characterizes certain forms of animal exploitation as different from, and worse than, other forms of exploitation and which suggests, by implication, that other forms of exploitation are acceptable. Both welfare campaigns and single-issue campaigns actually *promote* animal exploitation and result in partnerships between supposed animal advocates and institutionalized exploiters.

Principle Three

Abolitionists maintain that veganism is a moral baseline and that creative, nonviolent vegan education must be the cornerstone of rational animal rights advocacy.

Summary

Abolitionists embrace the idea that there is veganism and there is animal exploitation: there is no third choice. To not be a vegan is to participate directly in animal exploitation. Abolitionists promote veganism as a moral baseline or a moral imperative and as the *only* rational response to the recognition that animals have moral value. If animals matter morally, then we cannot treat them as commodities and eat, wear, or use them. Just as someone who promoted the abolition of slavery could not own slaves, an abolitionist with respect to animal slavery cannot consume animal products. For an abolitionist, veganism is a fundamental matter of justice. As the Abolitionist Approach is a grassroots movement, advocating veganism as a fundamental principle of justice is not something that requires large, wealthy charities and "leaders." It is something that we all can do and must do as a grassroots movement. Each of us must be a leader.

Principle Four

The Abolitionist Approach links the moral status of nonhumans with sentience alone and not with any other cognitive characteristic; all sentient beings are equal for the purpose of not being used exclusively as a resource.

Summary

Sentience is subjective awareness; there is some*one* who perceives and experiences the world. A sentient being has interests; that is, preferences, wants, or desires. If a being is sentient, then that is necessary and sufficient for the being to have the right not to be used as a means to human ends. The recognition of this right imposes on humans the moral obligation not to use that being as a resource. It is not necessary for a sentient being to have humanlike cognitive characteristics in order to be accorded the right not to be used as property.

Principle Five

Abolitionists reject all forms of human discrimination, including racism, sexism, heterosexism, ageism, ableism, and classism—just as they reject speciesism.

Summary

The Abolitionist Approach to Animal Rights rejects speciesism because, like racism, sexism, heterosexism, and other forms of human discrimination, it uses a morally irrelevant criterion (species) to discount and devalue the interests of sentient beings. But any opposition to speciesism makes sense *only* as part of a general opposition to all forms of discrimination. That is, we *cannot* oppose speciesism but claim that, as animal advocates, we do not have a position on these other forms of discrimination. We cannot say that we reject species as a morally objectionable criterion to discount or devalue the interests of nonhumans but that we do not have a position on whether race, sex, or sexual orientation/preference are morally objectionable criteria when used to discount or devalue human interests. Our opposition to speciesism *requires* that we oppose *all* discrimination.

Principle Six

Abolitionists recognize the principle of nonviolence as a core principle of the animal rights movement.

Summary

The Abolitionist Approach promotes nonviolence because it sees the animal rights movement as an extension of the peace movement to include concerns about nonhuman animals. Moreover, given that most people engage in animal exploitation, there is no principled way to distinguish exploiters for the purpose of justifying violence. Finally, because there is pervasive exploitation, violence cannot be understood as anything but a pathological reaction to what is regarded as normal. The only real option is, on the individual level, to embrace veganism as a moral baseline and, on the social level, to engage in creative, nonviolent vegan education from an abolitionist perspective.

Principle One

Abolitionists maintain that all sentient beings, human or nonhuman, have one right—the basic right not to be treated as the property of others.

Summary

Animals are classified as property and are used exclusively as resources for humans. Although we claim to regard animals as having moral value and to not be just things, their status as property means that they have no moral value; they have only economic value. We recognize that treating humans as property is inconsistent with recognizing humans as members of the moral community. We accept as a fundamental moral principle that all humans, irrespective of their particular characteristics, must be accorded the basic moral right not to be property. On this principle rests the universal condemnation of human slavery. The property status of animals means that animals are considered to be things, irrespective of what we say to the contrary. There is no way to distinguish humans from nonhumans that can justify withholding from all sentient nonhumans the same right that we accord to all humans. We need to recognize that all sentient beings are equal for the purpose of not being used exclusively as human resources. The Abolitionist Approach maintains that all animal use—however supposedly "humane"—is morally unjustified.

Discussion

Humans, Nonhumans, and Property

It is either the case that animals are *things*—that is, they have no moral value and we have no moral obligations that we owe to them—or they matter morally and we do have obligations that we owe to them.

We believe most people reject the idea that animals are things; on the contrary, they regard them as having moral value. Indeed, we would go further and say that many people feel a distinct sense of kinship with other animals.

The foundational principle of the Abolitionist Approach is that animals do matter morally and that this means we *must* recognize animals as holding one fundamental moral right—the right not to be used as property. That is, if animals matter morally—if they are not just things that have no moral value—then they *cannot* be property.

Why?

Because to be property *means* to be a thing that exists exclusively as a resource for others. To have the status of property is inconsistent with having moral value. To be property is to be *something,* not *someone.*

We recognize this in the human context and, as a result, we regard every human, despite their personal characteristics, as having a moral right not to be treated as property—a right to which we accord legal protection as well. This is another way of saying that we regard it morally odious to treat any human as a thing who exists exclusively as a resource for others. If we see why property status and moral value are incompatible in the human context, and why a right not to be treated as property is required, we will be able to see how this applies in the context of nonhumans.

But first, we need to understand what a right is.

What Is a Right?

Many people talk about rights without thinking about what they mean when they use the term. Throughout history, a great deal has been written about rights. It's a complicated topic in many ways, but, thankfully, we don't have to deal with most of it to understand what we need in order to make sense of the present discussion.

A right is simply a way of protecting an interest. An interest is something we prefer, desire, or want.

We all have interests; there are all sorts of things we prefer, desire, or want. Some of those interests are completely idiosyncratic. For example, some of us have an interest in playing golf; some have no interest whatsoever in playing golf. Some like rock music; others like classical. But some of our interests are shared and considered very important as social, cultural, and, perhaps, even spiritual matters. For example, our interests in freedom or liberty, free speech and thought, education, health care, basic nutrition, etc. are interests that matter to most of us and the way we protect those interests is central to our vision of what society should be.

There are two basic ways in which we can protect these important interests.

Those who subscribe to a *consequentialist* moral theory (of which there are different sorts) support protecting interests depending on whether the consequences of protecting those interests are better than the consequences of not protecting them. According to the primary form of consequentialist theory—*utilitarianism*—we ought to protect interests only to the extent that to do so will promote overall happiness, or pleasure, or the satisfaction of preferences of those affected. If overall happiness, or pleasure, or the satisfaction of preferences will be maximized if we don't protect the interest in question, we should not protect that interest.

Those who subscribe to a *rights* theory say that some interests are so important that we should protect them *irrespective* of consequences.

Let's consider an example: every person has an interest in their physical security. A rights theorist would say that this fundamental interest should be protected by a right and that we should not use a person as a non-consenting subject in a painful biomedical experiment in which they are ultimately killed even if their use might lead to a cure for a disease. A utilitarian would reject this and say that, other things being equal, we ought to use the human in the experiment because the consequences of finding a cure for cancer would outweigh the interest that the person has in their physical integrity: overall happiness, pleasure, or the satisfaction of preferences would be maximized if we use the non-consenting subject. Utilitarians would not acknowledge any claim of moral right on the part of the person being used in the experiment.

To say that an interest is protected by a right does not mean that we protect those interests absolutely. For example, not even the most fervent rights advocate would claim that a person's interest in liberty ought to be protected if that person is properly found guilty of committing a crime for which a prison sentence is the appropriate punishment. But an advocate of rights would not agree that the happiness or well-being of others can justify ignoring someone's interest in liberty. For example, some people maintain that our happiness or well-being justifies detaining people in places like Guantanamo Bay even though the detainees have never been found guilty of committing a crime. That is, those who support this detention maintain that the consequences of not protecting the fundamental interest of others in their liberty justify not protecting that interest. A rights advocate would disagree and would maintain that any good consequences that come from detaining people who have not been found guilty of any crime cannot justify ignoring this fundamental interest.

The Right of All Humans Not to Be Used as Property

Although there are some rights about which there is some agreement, there is a great deal of controversy and debate about which human interests should be protected as involving fundamental moral rights.

It may be safe to say that, with *one* exception, there is no single interest we *all* agree should, as a matter of fundamental morality, be protected by right. That one exception is that we all agree that human slavery is an abomination. When it comes to the human interest in not being the property of another— the interest in not being a replaceable resource who can be used and killed to benefit others—we agree that the interest at stake must be protected by a right. We might say that the interest in not being a replaceable resource is a *fundamental* interest. When a human is treated as a replaceable resource, that human is no longer a *person*. That human is a *thing.* "Person" used as a term in moral theory refers to someone who counts morally; someone whose interests must be given appropriate moral weight. A person is the opposite of a thing, which is an entity that has no moral value. If a human is property, that human is a thing. That human is placed *outside* the moral community.

Under race-based slavery in the United States, Africans were treated as chattel property. They did not have any inherent or intrinsic value but only had external or extrinsic value. They were things that were bought and sold, just as houses, land, carts, and cows were bought and sold. Some slave owners treated their slaves better than others. But that was because the slaves were property and the slave owners had the freedom to treat their slaves well, just as they had the freedom to treat them badly.

If a human is a slave or is otherwise treated as a replaceable resource, then that means that *someone else*—an owner, who can be an individual, a corporation or other similar entity, or the state itself—has the last word on how much the interests of that human are worth. Someone else, who has property rights in the slave, gets to determine how much the slave is worth. Someone else gets to value the fundamental interests that the slave has, including their fundamental interests in not suffering and in continuing to live, and has the ability to value those interests at *zero.* The law may impose certain limitations on how property may be treated, for example, by requiring that slaves be given sufficient food and water, but that is no different from the state requiring that you get your car inspected to make sure it's safe. A slave not only has no right not to be property but the slave owner also has a property right in the slave that allows the owner to value the slave's interests. To talk about balancing the interests of slaves against those of slave owners makes no sense whatsoever as it involves balancing the interests of a piece of property against those of a property owner who has property rights to value the slave as the owner determines.

We protect with a right the interest in not being treated as chattel property or exclusively as a resource for others. In other words, we protect this interest as a non-contingent matter irrespective of consequences. We do not think it is morally appropriate to treat humans as chattel slaves or as replaceable resources *even if* doing so would generate wonderful consequences for the rest of us. We could clearly kill and use healthy humans as forced organ donors and save at least 10 humans for every one we killed. But none of us would think that such a trade-off—although highly beneficial—would be morally acceptable.

We simply do not think that the interest that humans have in not being treated as things is the sort of interest that can be up for consequential grabs. We recognize that protecting this interest with a right is necessary, or else any human who does not hold this right will, by definition, be at risk of having all of their fundamental interests, including their interest in not suffering and their interest in their life, valued at zero. They will, by definition, no longer be a member of the moral community. They will literally be a thing that exists exclusively as a resource for others.

The right not to be treated as chattel property is a *minimum* standard for membership in the moral community. That is, if a human does not have this right, and can have all of their interests, including their interest in their life, valued at zero, then any other rights they might have are largely meaningless. If they can be used as a forced organ donor or as a non-consenting subject in a biomedical experiment, what difference does it make that they have a right of free speech or a right to vote?

The right not to be a slave is different from the right not to be the victim of discrimination. We may discriminate against humans in all sorts of ways and that is morally wrong but, unfortunately, there is a great deal of dispute about what constitutes discrimination. There is, however, *no* dispute about using humans as replaceable resources. When we do think of some sort of treatment as discriminatory, we condemn it. But enslaving humans is qualitatively worse than just about anything we can do to them. That is because when we are talking about discrimination, we are talking about discrimination against persons, or members of the moral community who should not be victims of discrimination. Discrimination involves not treating the similar interests of persons in a similar way. Discrimination is certainly not a good thing. But when we are talking about enslaving humans or otherwise treating them as replaceable resources, we have removed those humans *entirely* from the class of persons. We have placed them in the category of things.

We regard this right not to be a slave to be so important that every nation in the world has outlawed slavery. The right not to be a slave is one of the few rights recognized by the international community. This is not to say that human slavery no longer exists; it does. But no one defends it as they may defend other forms of what are arguably discrimination and exploitation. The right not to be treated as property is not accorded based on intelligence, athletic prowess, beauty, or any other personal characteristic. We enslave neither the brilliant surgeon nor the human who is mentally disabled. We may give greater compensation to a physicist than we do to someone who works as a janitor but we do not treat either exclusively as a resource.

In sum, although there is a great deal of disagreement about what human interests should be protected by rights, there is agreement that the interest in not being used as property should be protected in a non-contingent way—as a matter of right—irrespective of the personal characteristics of the particular human. If humans are chattel property, then they are no longer persons, or beings who count morally. They are merely things that have no inherent or intrinsic value; they only have whatever external or extrinsic value we decide to give them.

We can and do debate about whether other interests should be protected by rights. But we don't debate about human slavery. The interest in not being a slave is the very least that must be protected if a human is to be a member of the moral community at all.

The Right Not to Be Treated as Property: Nonhumans

Animals, like humans, have interests. Depending on the species we are talking about, and depending on individuals within that species ("animal" is a very broad term), those interests will vary. We may be uncertain whether some animals are sentient. For example, although insects clearly react to stimuli, it is not clear as to whether they are subjectively aware and able to experience pain and suffering. There may be uncertainty as to whether some mollusks, such as clams or oysters, are sentient. With regard to any unclear cases, we believe it prudent to err on the side of caution and regard close cases as being sentient. There is, however, absolutely no doubt that the animals we routinely exploit—cows, pigs, sheep, goats, chickens, turkeys, fish, lobsters, etc.—are sentient. All sentient beings have at least two interests: the interest in not suffering and the interest in not dying. That is, although not all sentient beings may think about their lives in the same way, all of them desire or want to remain alive. And the use of animals as property for food, clothing, and other purposes implicates at least two related, but different, interests that animals have. That is, using animals in the ways that we use them involves doing things to animals that they want, desire, or prefer us *not* to do: we cause them suffering and we kill them.

Just as in the case of human chattel slavery, if animals are property, *all* of their interests, from the most minor to the most fundamental, can be valued by someone else—a human owner—who has property rights in the animal and who may choose not to value that interest at all and who may ignore that interest. If animals are property, then animals have to hope that they have a "kind" owner, or else they will have a life that is largely determined by economics: their interests will be protected only when human owners find it financially beneficial to do so.

If animals are property, they are always at risk of having all of their interests ignored. And if animals are property, their interests will, as a general matter, be protected only when humans have an economic incentive to protect those interests. To talk about balancing the interests of nonhumans against those of humans is as nonsensical as it is to talk about balancing the interests of slaves against those of slave owners. Animals are property; humans have property rights in animals; there can be no balance of interests.

It is possible, of course, that some owners will treat their animals very well. Many of you reading this book may be sitting in a room with a companion animal who is happily sleeping away as you read. You love that dog or cat (or whatever the species) and regard them as a member of your family. But that animal is *your* property. Just as in the case of human slavery, you, as the owner, hold a property right in the animal that allows you to value that animal.

As a general matter, as long as we provide minimal food, water, and shelter, we can otherwise treat our animals pretty much as we choose. We can treat them as members of our family and lavish great affection on them. Or we can use them as guard dogs and never let them into the house or show them any affection. They are our property. They are things that we own. *We* get to value their every interest. *We* get to decide every aspect of their lives. *We* get to decide if they live or die. *We* have the legal right to dump our animals at a "shelter" where they may be killed. *We* have the right to have a veterinarian kill the animal. In most places, we can kill our animals ourselves as long as we do it "humanely."

One of the characteristics of property ownership is that the owner gets to decide how much to value their property. For instance, Mary owns a car. She can choose to take very good care of her car, and service it often, or she can do the bare minimum so that it passes inspection. It's *her* car to do with as she pleases.

The very same analysis holds for Mary's dog, Spot.

Mary may choose to treat Spot as a member of the family, take him for regular veterinary visits, groom him frequently, feed him high-quality food, and show him a great deal of affection. Alternatively, Mary can use Spot as a guard dog and never allow him in the house and never show him a minute of affection. As long as she provides sufficient food, water, and shelter to keep Spot alive, and makes sure he has his rabies shot, Mary can otherwise ignore Spot completely and not value any of his other interests, including his need for interaction and affection. Spot is *her* dog to do with as she pleases.

So if an animal is property, that animal is entirely at the mercy of others who get to decide the value of that animal. The law may limit the ways in which the animal property can be treated, just as the law can require that you provide sufficient maintenance to your car so that it passes inspection. But, ultimately, if something is property, it is a thing whose value is determined by someone else.

Treating Similar Cases Similarly: The Principle of Equal Consideration

Animals have interests in not being used in the many ways in which we use them and in which we use no humans. They have interests in not suffering and in not being killed. We recognize that if humans are not to be considered as things, we must accord them at least one right: the right not to be chattel property; the right not to be a replaceable resource. And although we argue endlessly about human rights, we all agree that humans should not be used exclusively as replaceable resources. But we do not extend this one right to nonhumans. If animals matter morally, then we must follow the basic moral rule—the principle of equal consideration—which stands for a very simple idea: treat like cases alike. We must accord to animals the same right that we accord to all humans unless there is a good reason not to do so.

Do we have a good reason not to do so? The short answer is, "no."

Most people think that a good reason not to accord to nonhumans the one right we accord to all humans is that humans and nonhumans may be similar in that both suffer, but they are different because nonhumans are intellectually less sophisticated than humans. We can write symphonies and poems, and we can build skyscrapers. Nonhumans can't. Therefore, we are "higher" forms of life.

Putting aside that many of us can't write symphonies or poems, or don't have any engineering skills, and also putting aside that many of us use our abilities to write hateful screeds and build weapons, why do we think that our cognitive capacities are more morally valuable than the characteristics animals have? Why do we think that someone who can do mathematics is more morally valuable for the purpose of determining who can be used as a resource and treated as a thing than someone who can soar in flight or who can hear or smell things that no human can?

That's easy. *We* do the valuing and we value what *we* are. We can use symbolic communication (language) and can do mathematics but we cannot fly, or breathe underwater, or do many of the things that animals can do. So we say that our ability to use language and do mathematics makes us special.

But the notion that supposedly more sophisticated intellectual abilities translate into greater moral value for all purposes—particularly for the purpose of determining whom we can morally justify using as a thing exclusively for the benefit of others—can be a *very* problematic idea.

Let's look at an example involving humans: Mary is a brilliant mathematician. John not only lacks math ability but suffers from a general and severe mental disability that makes him unable to add 2 + 2. Is Mary's cognitive superiority relevant to how we treat John?

It may be. It depends on the particular question we're asking. If the question is who—John or Mary—should be hired as a math teacher, the answer is clear: John's cognitive deficit is relevant. We should hire Mary.

Indeed, given the severity of John's condition, we most likely will also not allow him to drive, to enter into contracts, to write a check, or to have a credit card, and we may require that a guardian be appointed by a court to manage John's affairs.

So John's lesser ability *may* be relevant and we *may* deny him many of the opportunities that we provide to normal humans. His lesser ability may, of course, also mean that, for certain purposes, we favor him. For example, because John is not able to care for himself, we may provide public assistance to him that we would not provide to Mary.

But what if the question is different? What if we are asking whether John's disability is relevant to whether we should use him as a replaceable resource whose life should be "sacrificed" for others? What if the question is whom should we use as a replaceable resource—as, in effect, a *slave*—to serve the interests of others?

When the question changes from who gets a driver's license to who gets enslaved, or otherwise treated exclusively as a resource, we see immediately that the answer changes. Cognitive capacities may be relevant to who gets a particular job or driver's license or who is permitted to write checks, have a credit card, or enter into contracts. We may give a greater share of social resources (in the form of employment opportunities and salary) to Mary, but that does not mean that we can treat John as a thing. Cognitive capacities are not relevant to the matter of whom we enslave, use as a forced organ donor, or otherwise treat exclusively as a resource. We should use neither John nor Mary as a replaceable resource. If humans have any moral value at all—if they have any value beyond their extrinsic value as commodities valued by others—then, *whatever* other rights we may give humans, we *must* give them the basic right not to be the property or resources of others.

Similarly, the fact that nonhumans may be cognitively different from humans may be relevant for some purposes, but that difference can no more justify treating a sentient nonhuman exclusively as a resource for humans than it can justify treating a mentally disabled human exclusively as a resource for other humans. Mental disability may justify different treatment in some circumstances but not when it comes to whether it is morally acceptable to use the disabled human as a resource for others.

It really does not matter what the supposed cognitive difference between humans and nonhumans is—rational thought, the use of abstract concepts or symbolic communication, or the ability to engage in reciprocal moral behavior. The analysis is the same. The fact that nonhumans cannot recognize or act in response to moral obligations is irrelevant to whether they have the moral right not to be treated as things. We see this easily where humans are concerned. We may not allow a human who cannot understand or act on obligations to make a contract, or think that it is likely that they will make good on any promise, but we recognize that such a characteristic has absolutely no relevance to whether it is morally acceptable to use such a human as a forced organ donor or slave.

There are certainly differences between the minds of humans and the minds of nonhumans. But just as a human disability may be relevant for some purposes and yet have no relevance to whether we should use that disabled human as a slave, the fact that animals may not have certain cognitive capacities is not relevant to whether we should treat them as things. If animals have moral value, we can't use them as things. To do so would be to deny their moral status, which we claim to embrace. To recognize that we cannot treat any sentient human being (irrespective of other characteristics) exclusively as a resource, but to think that we can treat nonhumans who are sentient exclusively as a resource is nothing more than *speciesism*—a form of discrimination that allows us to devalue the interests of nonhumans based solely on species. Speciesism is like racism (which allows us to devalue the interests of humans based solely on race), sexism (which allows that devaluation based solely on sex), heterosexism (where the devaluation is based on sexual preference or orientation), or classism (where a person's economic class alone is used to justify excluding or limiting that person from full membership in the moral community). In the case of nonhuman animals, we not only accord less protection to their interests based on species, but we do not even recognize that they have an interest in living and we maintain the right to use and kill them in situations in which we would not think it appropriate to use or kill any humans.

The Abolitionist Approach: Abolition and Equality

The Abolitionist Approach maintains that, just as recognizing the moral value of humans requires that we abolish human slavery, recognizing the moral value of nonhumans similarly requires that we abolish the institutionalized exploitation of animals. We are morally obligated to stop treating animals as commodities. We are morally obligated to recognize that all sentient beings are equal for the purpose of not being used exclusively as resources. This does not mean that we need to treat humans and animals the same just as we do not treat all humans the same. We may pay a surgeon more than we pay a janitor. We may refuse to give a severely mentally disabled person a driving license. In certain cases, different characteristics can justify different treatment. Humans are not equal for all purposes. But when it comes to deciding whom we should enslave, or whom we should use as a non-consenting subject in a biomedical experiment, all humans are equal; we should not enslave any of them or use any of them exclusively as resources for others.

Similarly, to say that nonhumans and humans are moral equals is not to say that we should give nonhumans the right to vote or to drive cars. There are clearly differences between humans and nonhumans that justify different treatment in some circumstances. But, for the purposes of being treated as property, as a resource for others, all sentient beings are equal. None should be used as property. None should be used exclusively as resources for others.

If we recognize that nonhuman animals have the fundamental right not to be treated as resources, then we can no longer justify using animals for food, clothing, entertainment, experiments, etc. We must *abolish* the institutionalized exploitation of nonhuman animals.

As we will see in our discussion of *Principle Two,* there are some so-called animal advocates who maintain that, for purposes of having a right not to be used as replaceable resources, humans and nonhumans are differently situated; therefore, the principle of equal consideration does not require that we recognize that animals have a right not to be used as property. These advocates claim that animals don't care *that* we use them; they only care about *how* we use them. They claim that animals are not self-aware and do not have an interest in continuing to live; that they only have an interest in having a reasonably pleasant life and a relatively painless death. Therefore, according to these advocates, if we treat animals "well," our use of animals is not per se objectionable. This is known as the *animal welfare* position and it has a number of different formulations. As we will see, the Abolitionist Approach rejects the view that sentient nonhumans do not have an interest in continuing to live and maintains that animal use is morally objectionable even if the treatment of animals is "humane."

It is, of course, better to inflict less pain and suffering than more, but that does not mean that the morality of an institution is determined by issues of treatment. For example, we would all agree that beating one's slaves less is better than beating one's slaves more, but the institution of slavery is still morally wrong. Treating one's slaves more "humanely" does not make the institution of slavery any more morally acceptable. No one would promote the "humane" treatment of slaves as something that would eradicate the injustice of the institution of slavery. The "humane" treatment of animals similarly does not eradicate the injustice of the institution of animal slavery.

The Right Not to Be Property and Domestication

To say that an animal has a right not to be used as property is simply to say that we have a moral obligation to not use animals as things even if it would benefit us to do so. With respect to domesticated animals, that means that we stop bringing them into existence altogether. So in this sense, the right not to be used as property arguably has a different result when it is applied to nonhumans than when it is applied to humans. In the latter case, the abolition of slavery means that those who were enslaved are no longer slaves and they became full members of the moral community. In the former case, it means that we care for those domesticated nonhumans currently in existence but we do not bring any more into existence. So recognizing the right not to treat animals as property means that we don't perpetuate domestication. We acknowledge that this may be an ostensibly odd use of "right" in that, if the right is respected, the nonhuman rightholders will cease to exist. If we recognized that animals should be accorded this moral right, then we would be morally obligated to care for all domesticated nonhumans now in existence. But we would be under an obligation not to bring any more into existence and the basis of that obligation would be that, were we to do so, it would violate the right of nonhumans. This is similar to the human context: we are under an obligation not to enslave people because that would violate the right not to be property of those we enslave.

But what if we wished to bring animals into existence and not use them exclusively as resources? That is, what if we wanted to bring domesticated animals into existence who we did not use and kill for our purposes? The obvious situation that comes to mind is whether it would be morally acceptable to continue to breed animals, like dogs and cats, who live with us as "pets."

The Abolitionist Approach maintains that such continued domestication is not morally acceptable. Although some of us treat our companion animals as family members, some of us do not. But however we treat our dogs, cats, etc., they are property as far as the law is concerned. If you regard your dog as a member of your family and treat her well, the law will protect your decision just as it will protect your decision to change the oil in your car every 1000 miles—the dog and the car are your property and if you wish to accord a higher value to your property, the law will allow you to do so. But if you wish to accord your property a lower value and, for instance, have a guard dog whom you keep chained in your yard and to whom you provide minimal food, water, and shelter, and no companionship or affection, the law will protect that decision as well.

The reality is that in the United States, most dogs and cats do not end up dying of old age in loving homes. Most have homes for a relatively short period of time before they are transferred to another owner, taken to a shelter, dumped, or taken to a veterinarian to be killed.

And it does not matter whether we characterize an owner as a "guardian," as some advocates urge. Such a characterization is meaningless. If you have the legal right to take your dog to a kill shelter, or to a veterinarian to be killed, or to "humanely" kill your dog yourself, it does not matter what you call your dog. Your dog is your property. Those of us who live with companion animals are owners as far as the law is concerned and we have the legal right to treat our animals as we see fit with few limitations. Anticruelty laws do not even apply to the vast majority of instances in which humans inflict cruel treatment on nonhumans.

But we could, at least in theory, have a different and more acceptable relationship with nonhumans. What if we abolished the property status of animals and required that we treat dogs and cats similar to the way we treat human children? For instance, what if humans who lived with dogs could not treat them as property and *had* to treat them as family members? What if humans could not kill nonhuman companions except in instances in which at least some of us would regard it as acceptable to allow assisted suicide in the human context (e.g., when the human is incurably ill and in great pain). This position—that we can continue to bring domesticated animals into existence but not treat them as property—is referred to as the "citizenship" position. Would it be acceptable to continue to breed nonhumans to be our companions then?

The answer is, "no."

Putting aside that the development of general standards of what would constitute treating nonhumans as "family members" and the resolution of all the related issues would be impossible as a practical matter, this position neglects to recognize that domestication itself raises serious moral issues irrespective of *how* the nonhumans involved are treated.

Domesticated animals are dependent on us for when and whether they eat, whether they have water, where and when they urinate, when they sleep, whether they get any exercise, etc. Unlike human children, who, except in unusual cases, will become independent and functioning members of human society, domestic animals are neither part of the nonhuman world nor fully part of our world. They remain forever in a netherworld of vulnerability, dependent on us for everything that is of relevance to them. We have bred them to be compliant and servile, or to have characteristics that are actually harmful to them but are pleasing to us. We may make them happy in one sense, but the relationship can never be "natural" or "normal." They do not belong stuck in our world irrespective of how well we treat them.

This is more or less true of all domesticated nonhumans. They are perpetually dependent on us. We control their lives forever. They truly are "animal slaves." We may be benevolent masters, but we really aren't anything more than that. And that cannot be right.

We live with six rescued dogs. All six would be dead if we had not adopted them. We love them very much and try very hard to provide them with the best of care and treatment. (And before anyone asks, all eight of us are vegans!) You would probably not find two people on the planet who enjoy living with dogs more than we do.

But if there were two dogs left in the universe and it were up to us as to whether they were allowed to breed so that we could continue to live with dogs, and even if we could guarantee that all dogs would have homes as loving as the one that we provide, we would not hesitate for a second to bring the whole institution of "pet" ownership to an end. We regard the dogs who live with us as refugees of sorts, and although we enjoy caring for them, it is clear that humans have no business continuing to bring these creatures into a world in which they simply do not fit.

There are those who think that "animal rights" means that nonhumans have some sort of right to reproduce, and it is therefore wrong to sterilize nonhumans. If that view were correct, then we would be morally committed to allowing all domesticated species to continue to reproduce indefinitely. We could not limit this "right of reproduction" to dogs and cats alone. Moreover, it makes no sense to say that we have acted immorally in domesticating nonhuman animals but that we are now committed to allowing them to continue to breed. We made a moral mistake by domesticating nonhumans in the first place; what sense does it make to perpetuate it?

There are some who claim that we will lose "diversity" if we no longer have these domesticated nonhumans. Even if continued domestication were necessary for biological diversity, that would not mean that it would be morally acceptable. We do not, however, have to address that issue. There is nothing "natural" about domesticated animals. They are creatures we have created through selective breeding and confinement and who cannot survive independently in the wild. To the extent that they have undomesticated relatives living in nature, we should certainly seek to protect those nonhumans first and foremost for their own sake and secondarily for the purposes of biological diversity. But our protection of presently existing domesticated nonhumans is not necessary for any sort of biological diversity.

With respect to non-domesticated nonhumans, recognizing their right not to be used as property means that we do not hunt them and we endeavor to act without harming them in any way. Otherwise, we are not in favor of human attempts to manipulate the environment for the supposed benefit of nonhumans. Humans have a rather poor track record in this regard.

Some animal advocates claim that the Abolitionist Approach is a theory of negative rights alone; that is, they claim that it recognizes only a right not to be used as property and that it does not recognize positive rights. This observation is correct but it must be remembered that if we recognized this one right, *all* domestication would end. We would be obligated to care for those domesticated animals now in existence, but we would bring no more into existence. During this period of transition, our changed view of the personhood of animals would obviate the necessity of restricting the treatment of animals as required when animals are viewed as resources. If we all embraced the personhood of nonhumans, we would need to think about rights to address issues that arise in connection with our interaction with non-domesticated animals who live among us and in undeveloped areas. But if we were beings who cared enough to not eat, wear, or otherwise use domesticated nonhumans, we would undoubtedly be able to figure out what those additional rights would be. The most important thing is that we recognize the negative right not to be used as property, which requires the abolition of institutions that allow for the commodification and control of animals by humans.

Conclusion

Most people think that animals matter morally—that they are not just things that exist exclusively as resources for humans. But despite this widely shared moral view, we nevertheless use animals as resources. That is because despite what we say about our moral views regarding animals, the social, legal, and economic reality is that animals are just property. If animals are property, all they can be is just things. To be property *means* to be a thing excluded from the moral community.

We recognized this where humans were concerned. We recognized that if humans were property—if they were chattel slaves—they could not be members of the moral community. They could not be moral persons; they could only be things. We now accept that every human being—whatever their level of intelligence, talent, beauty, etc.—holds a pre-legal moral right not to be treated as property. They have the right to be a moral person and not a thing.

Yet, we have not extended this right to animals. The principle of equal consideration says that we must treat similar interests similarly. Both humans and nonhumans have an interest in not being treated exclusively as resources. We accord a right not to be used as a resource to humans but we do not accord that right to nonhumans. This different treatment is speciesist and abolitionists reject it.

Recognizing this one right means that we can no longer justify exploiting animals for human purposes. We are obligated to *abolish* animal exploitation, which rests on the notion that animals are things. The Abolitionist Approach rejects the idea that we can use animals as long as we treat them "humanely." We will turn to that discussion in the next chapter.

Further Reading

Books

Gary L. Francione, *Introduction to Animal Rights: Your Child or the Dog?* (Temple University Press 2000).

Essays

Gary L. Francione, "Animals – Property or Persons?" in Cass R. Sunstein and Martha C. Nussbaum, editors, *Animal Rights: Current Debates and New Directions* (Oxford University Press, 2004) 108-142, and reprinted in Gary L. Francione, *Animals as Persons: Essays in the Abolition of Animal Exploitation* (Columbia University Press, 2008) 25-66.

Gary L. Francione and Anna E. Charlton, "Animal Advocacy in the 21st Century: The Abolition of the Property Status of Nonhumans" in Taimie L. Bryant, Rebecca J. Huss, and David N. Cassuto, editors, *Animal Law and the Courts: A Reader* (Thomson/West Publishing, 2008) 7-35.

Gary Francione, "One Right for All," *New Scientist,* October 8, 2005, available at www.abolitionistapproach.com/media/pdf/one_right_for_all-newscientist.pdf

Blog Posts

Clarifying the Meaning of 'Right,'" at www.abolitionistapproach.com/clarifying-the-meaning-of-a-right

"'Pets': The Inherent Problems of Domestication," at www.abolitionistapproach.com/pets-the-inherent-problems-of-domestication

"Animal Rights and Domesticated Nonhumans," at www.abolitionistapproach.com/animal-rights-and-domesticated-nonhumans

Principle Two

Abolitionists maintain that our recognition of this one basic right means that we must abolish, and not merely regulate, institutionalized animal exploitation, and that abolitionists should not support welfare reform campaigns or single-issue campaigns.

Summary

Recognizing the right of animals not to be used as property requires that we abolish the institutionalized exploitation of nonhuman animals, and not just regulate it to make it more "humane." Abolitionists reject animal welfare campaigns. They also reject single-issue campaigns, a particular sort of regulatory campaign that characterizes certain forms of animal exploitation as different from, and worse than, other forms of exploitation and which suggests, by implication, that other forms of exploitation are acceptable. Both welfare campaigns and single-issue campaigns actually *promote* animal exploitation and result in partnerships between supposed animal advocates and institutionalized exploiters.

Discussion

Abolitionists Reject the Welfarist Position

The Abolitionist Approach maintains that if we reject the idea that animals are things, we must recognize that they have a fundamental right not to be used as property. This requires that we reject the institutions of animal use for food, clothing, entertainment, experiments, etc., and that we abolish this institutionalized exploitation.

But what about the position that we can still use animals as long as we treat them "humanely"? That is known as the *animal welfare* position. Abolitionists explicitly and unequivocally reject the animal welfare position.

But isn't less suffering better than more suffering? Of course it is. But imposing less suffering does not address the fundamental injustice of animal use. As we saw in the context of human slavery: it is better to beat the slaves less than more, but beating the slaves less does not address the fundamental injustice of slavery. Just as abolitionists with respect to slavery rejected human slavery—however "humane" the treatment of slaves—abolitionists with respect to nonhuman exploitation maintain that we cannot justify animal slavery, however "humane" it may be.

The welfarist position focuses on treatment and not use, and maintains that use is not the primary issue, or that it may not be an issue at all, as long as treatment is "humane." The Abolitionist Approach focuses on use and not treatment, and maintains that we cannot morally justify *any* animal use.

Welfarists may or may not see animal slavery that is more "humane" as a means to the end of abolishing animal use. That is, some welfarists may see exploitation that is more "humane" as the ultimate goal. They have no problem with animal use per se, and think that it is morally unobjectionable that humans use and kill nonhumans as long as they treat them "humanely"

32

and do not impose "unnecessary" suffering on them. These welfarists see the regulation of animal exploitation as an end in itself.

Other welfarists, however, may claim to want to end animal use altogether at some point in the distant future, or, at least, to reduce significantly the number of animals exploited by humans, but they promote "humane" animal exploitation and other forms of regulation as a supposed means to that end. We call those welfarists in the second group *new welfarists* because they promote "humane" animal exploitation but they do so supposedly as a means to some other end and not as an end in itself. Most of the large animal organizations now subscribe to some version of new welfarism. Many of these groups claim to want to abolish animal exploitation at some point in the future and they argue that treatment that is supposedly more "humane" is a means to that end.

But regardless of whether they are traditional welfarists or new welfarists, *all* welfarists support the regulation of animal exploitation and they characterize "humane" exploitation as a morally good thing. By doing so, they *necessarily* promote and encourage supposedly "humane" animal exploitation.

The theoretical basis of the animal welfare position is the view that animals do not care *that* we use or kill them; they care only about *how* we treat them and kill them. According to this view, animals live in an eternal present and have no interest per se in continuing to live. They only have an interest in not suffering pain, distress, and fear. We will explore briefly the origin of the welfarist position and its promotion by modern "animal advocacy" organizations. We will then go on to examine the reasons why it is unequivocally rejected by the Abolitionist Approach.

The Origin of the Welfarist Position

The welfarist position emerged in the early nineteenth century as a rejection of the idea that animals were things that had no moral value whatsoever because they were less sophisticated mentally than humans (they could not reason, use abstractions, speak, etc.) or because they were not made in the "image of God," as humans supposedly were. Reformers of that period, such as Jeremy Bentham and John Stuart Mill, argued that as long as animals could suffer, humans had a moral obligation that they owed to animals to give weight to animal interests in not suffering. As Bentham stated in this often-quoted passage, "the question is not, Can they *reason*? nor, Can they *talk*? but, Can they *suffer*?"[1]

Although the welfarist position in many ways represented a paradigm shift relative to earlier thinking about animals (welfarists recognized animals as having moral value and not as being mere things), welfarists did not reject most animal use, and, in particular, did not reject the use of animals for food. Indeed, they made very clear that the use of animals for food, which represents, by far, our most numerically significant use of animals, was fine. According to the early welfarists, animals are not self-aware. That is, they do not have the sort of reflective self-consciousness that humans have. They do not care *that* we use and kill them; they care only about *how* we treat them and kill them. According to Bentham, if we kill and eat animals, "we are the better for it, and they are never the worse. They have none of those long-protracted anticipations of future misery which we have." Bentham also maintained that we actually do animals a favor by killing them, as long as we do so in a relatively painless manner, "The death they suffer in our hands commonly is, and always may be, a speedier, and by that means a less painful one, than that which would await them in the inevitable course of nature. . . . [W]e should be the worse for their living, and they are never the worse for being dead."

This notion that animals do not have an interest in continuing to live set the stage for the idea that it is acceptable to use and kill animals as long as we regulate animal use to make sure that it is "humane;" and this resulted in the anticruelty laws and other laws that we have today.

---

[1] This and following quotes from Bentham are from Jeremy Bentham, *An Introduction to the Principles of Morals and Legislation* (New York: Hafner 1948), at 310-11, n.1.

Peter Singer and the "Animal Liberation" Approach

The welfarist idea that animals do not have an interest in continuing to live is at the core of Peter Singer's "Animal Liberation" philosophy, which is embraced by just about all of the large animal organizations.[2] Singer, like Bentham, believes that most animals are not self-aware in the way that "normal" humans are. According to Singer, they are not forward-looking and do not have hopes and desires for the future; unlike humans, who not only have an interest in not suffering but also have an interest in continuing to live. So if Joe sneaks into Tom's room while Tom is sleeping and kills him instantly and without pain with a single bullet to the brain, Tom has still been harmed even if he does not suffer. Tom is self-aware and "has a life." He is forward-looking. Joe's killing Tom has prevented Tom from doing what he planned to do and satisfying his future-oriented desires.

According to Singer, nonhuman animals (or most of them at least) do not "have a life" in the sense of having any continuity of consciousness over time. They are not self-aware or forward-looking in the way that humans are. They live in a sort of "eternal present" and they do not care *that* we use and kill them for our purposes; they just care about *how* we treat them and how we kill them. He maintains that, as long as we take their interests in not suffering seriously, we can continue to use animals. A painless death is not a harm as far as animals are concerned. As Singer has stated plainly, "There might be some people who say, 'You can't be compassionate if you end up killing the animals.' I just think that's wrong. . . . I think as long as the standards really are compassionate ones, that do as much as they can to give the animals decent lives before they're killed, I don't have a problem with it."[3]

It should be noted that Singer, like Bentham, is a utilitarian. Utilitarians are consequentialists who, as we saw in our discussion of *Principle One,* reject the notion of moral rights altogether because they believe that the interests of nonhumans and humans should be protected only if the consequences

---

[2] See Peter Singer, *Animal Liberation,* rev. ed. (New York: New York Review of Books 1990); Peter Singer, *Practical Ethics,* 3d ed. (New York: Cambridge University Press 2011).
[3] http://www.satyamag.com/oct06/singer.html

weigh in favor of doing so. Specifically, utilitarians maintain that we should protect interests only if doing so will produce better consequences (happiness, pleasure, satisfaction of interests, etc.) than not doing so. It is, indeed, irony of a grand sort that Peter Singer, the so-called "father of the animal rights movement," denies that animals have rights at all.

Although Bentham and Singer reject the notion of moral rights for humans as well, both reject human slavery. Bentham rejected slavery at least in part because he realized that to be a slave was to be a thing that existed outside the moral community. So although Bentham rejected rights, he accorded rights-type protection to the interest of humans in not being chattel property and opposed all human slavery. Similarly, although Singer rejects moral rights, he also maintains that we should not treat at least normal humans as replaceable resources. He views normal humans, who are self-aware and are forward-looking, with hopes and desires for the future, as individuals with unique value. He believes that such humans cannot be easily replaced because of their unique value. That value may be overridden by consequences in a particular situation, but this presumption of unique value acts to provide rights-type protection in many instances. In any event, although Bentham and Singer deny that humans have moral rights, they extend rights-type protection to humans when it comes to using humans as replaceable resources.

Bentham and Singer do not extend this rights-type protection to nonhumans because they view humans and nonhumans as relevantly dissimilar and neither sees anything wrong per se with humans owning and using animals. A truly "compassionate" and "humane" system of animal slavery would be morally defensible because animals, unlike humans, are not self-aware and they live in a sort of "eternal present." They do not care that we use them and kill them. They care only about how we treat them and how we kill them. For Bentham and Singer, if we provided a wonderful life to nonhumans and killed them painlessly, we would be doing nothing wrong.

Types of Animal Welfare and Regulation

The welfarist position is reflected in our conventional thinking about animal ethics. That is, most people on the street think that animals matter morally to some degree and reject the idea that animals are just things that don't matter morally at all. They may, as is almost always the case, think that animals matter less than humans do, but they think that animals matter to some extent. Most people think that it is acceptable to use and kill animals for human purposes as long as we treat them "humanely" and do not impose "unnecessary" suffering on them. These moral ideas are reflected in laws, such as anticruelty laws.

But the animal welfare position is also the position of *all* of the large animal advocacy organizations in North America, South America, Australasia, and Europe. That is, virtually all of these organizations follow Singer's approach and focus on the treatment of animals. None of them promotes the idea that any use of animals as replaceable resources—however "humane"—is morally wrong. They promote regulatory campaigns to make treatment more "humane" or "compassionate." Some of these organizations adopt a traditional welfarist approach and maintain that animal use is morally acceptable. These organizations see regulation as an end in itself. Such organizations include the Humane Society of the United States (HSUS), the Animal Welfare Institute, the Royal Society for the Prevention of Cruelty to Animals (RSPCA), and Compassion in World Farming (CIWF). Other organizations adopt a new welfarist position and claim to value regulation as a means to an end in that regulation will at some point in an undefined distant future lead to the end of animal exploitation or, at the very least, to a reduction in the number of animals who are exploited. New welfarist organizations include People for the Ethical Treatment of Animals (PETA), Farm Sanctuary, Animal Aid, and Viva!.

Regulatory campaigns come in two primary forms. There are *animal welfare reform campaigns* that supposedly seek to make animal exploitation more "humane." These sorts of campaigns may seek legislative change in the form of a law or amendments to an existing law, or they may seek to persuade industry to make voluntary reforms apart from any legal requirement. Examples of welfare campaigns include efforts to phase out the gestation crate for pigs, obtain larger cages for laying hens or for animals used in biomedical experiments, or to adopt supposedly more "humane" methods of slaughter.

There are also *single-issue campaigns,* or "SICs," that target particular animal products or animal uses, and advocate for the abolition of those products or uses but not for the abolition of animal exploitation generally. That is, SICs do not generally advocate that their target be done or produced more "humanely," but rather, that it not be done or produced at all. Examples of SICs include the anti-fur campaign, campaigns against the consumption of dogs and cats in Asia, campaigns for special protection for certain animals who are thought to be cognitively similar to humans (nonhuman great apes or dolphins) or who are otherwise thought to be "special" in some sense, and campaigns against the use of chickens in ritual slaughter by Hassidic Jews. Although SICs are often characterized as seeking to "abolish" certain forms of exploitation, in reality, they merely promote the idea that certain forms of animal exploitation are to be preferred as morally acceptable.

Abolitionists unequivocally reject animal reform campaigns and SICs. In the next section, we will explore the reasons for this rejection.

Why Abolitionists Reject Welfare Reform and SICs

As a general matter, abolitionists reject welfare reform for one simple reason: if we cannot justify animal exploitation at all, it makes no sense to campaign for animal exploitation, even if it is supposedly more "humane." If animal exploitation is wrong, we should not encourage people to do the wrong thing. That said, we will explore six specific reasons why abolitionists reject welfare reform campaigns and SICs.

First, abolitionists reject the idea that animals do not have an interest in continuing to live that is distinct from an interest in not suffering.

As previously discussed, the very basis of the welfarist position as a historical matter is that animals are not self-aware and that they live in an "eternal present." They supposedly do not care that we use them but only care about how we treat them. Abolitionists reject this notion and maintain that it rests on a species-biased (or speciesist) notion of what it means to be self-aware, and they reject the idea that nonhuman animals do not care if we kill and use them as long as we kill them painlessly. To say that a sentient being—any sentient being—is not harmed by death is decidedly odd. After all, sentience is not something that has evolved to serve as an end in itself. Rather, it is a trait that allows the beings who have it to identify situations that are harmful and that threaten survival. *Sentience is a means to the end of continued existence.* Sentient beings, simply by virtue of their being sentient, have an interest in remaining alive; that is, they prefer, want, or desire to remain alive. The Jains of India expressed it well long ago, "All beings are fond of life, like pleasure, hate pain, shun destruction, like life, long to live. To all life is dear."[4]

Therefore, to say that a sentient being is not harmed by death denies that the being has the very interest that sentience serves to perpetuate. It would be analogous to saying that a being with eyes does not have an interest in continuing to see or is not harmed by being made blind. We agree with the

---

[4] *Acharanga Sutra,* 1.2.3.

late Donald Griffin, a biologist and one of the foremost ethologists of the twentieth century, who noted that although nonhumans may not be able to think of themselves in the autobiographical ways that humans do, that does not mean that nonhumans are not, on some level, aware of themselves.[5] It would seem that any sentient being must be self-aware in that to be sentient means to be the sort of being who recognizes that it is *that being,* and not some other, who is experiencing pain or distress; there is some*one* who is conscious of being in pain and who has a preference or desire not to have that experience.

We do not believe that most animals are confined to an "eternal present" and we would guess that those who share their home with a dog, cat, or other nonhuman would also not agree with this notion. But we think that, even if this were the case and animals were stuck in the present, this would not mean that animals are not self-aware. Consider humans who have a form of amnesia called "transient global amnesia." These people are often unable to remember the past or plan for the future, but have a sense of themselves in the present time and place. Their sense of self-awareness may be different from that of a normal adult, but it would not be accurate to say that they are not self-aware, or that they are indifferent to death, or that death is not a harm to them. Someone with such amnesia, who may be said to be confined to an "eternal present," still has some forward-looking thinking in that they are anticipating the next second of existence.

We may not want to appoint such a person as a teacher or allow them to perform surgery on others, but most of us would be horrified at the suggestion that it is acceptable to use such people as forced organ donors or as non-consenting subjects in biomedical experiments, even if we did so "humanely." Even if animals lived in a similar "eternal present" (a notion we reject as absurd), that would not mean that they are not self-aware, that they have no interest in continued existence, or that death is not a harm for them.

We will discuss this topic more when we come to *Principle Four,* but it will suffice for present purposes to say that abolitionists maintain that all sentient beings value their lives and that killing animals, however "humanely," imposes a harm on them.

---

[5] See Donald R. Griffin, *Animal Minds: Beyond Cognition to Consciousness* (Chicago: University of Chicago Press 2001), at 274.

Second, welfare reform campaigns and SICs *necessarily* promote animal exploitation.

The purpose of welfare reform campaigns and SICs is to build coalitions that include those who believe that animal exploitation per se is morally acceptable and who just object to the target of the particular welfare reform campaign or SIC. Such campaigns *must* play to the lowest level of the spectrum or they will lose that part of the coalition.

And that is precisely the problem.

A welfare reform campaign that aims to phase out gestation crates for pigs seeks to build a coalition that includes people who eat animal products, including pork, but who agree that the gestation crate is not "humane." A welfare reform campaign that aims to phase out the traditional battery cage for laying hens seeks to build a coalition that includes people who eat eggs from hens confined in an "enriched" cage or in one big cage known as a "cage-free" barn. An SIC that targets foie gras seeks to build a coalition that will include people who eat meat but who think that foie gras is morally distinguishable from other meat. An SIC that targets meat seeks to build a coalition that will include people who consume dairy and eggs. An SIC that targets fur seeks to build a coalition of people who wear wool, leather, or silk instead of fur.

Because welfare reform campaigns and SICs seek to build coalitions of people, many of whom engage in conduct that is indistinguishable from the target of the particular welfare reform campaign or SIC that they are supporting, these campaigns *necessarily* promote the animal exploitation that is not the target of that welfare campaign or that SIC. That is, the reform campaign *must* characterize the reform of the use or the products that are not the target of the SIC (but are morally indistinguishable from it), as more "humane" or "compassionate," not just as a factual matter (it supposedly causes less suffering), *but as a normative or moral matter*. In other words, welfare reform campaigns and SICs communicate to the public that the supposedly reformed use or the non-targeted product is what people *ought* to support.

So a campaign against the gestation crate *must* promote non-crate pork as a normatively desirable choice—as what people *ought* to support and consume. If the campaign even suggested that all meat consumption or even all pork consumption was morally wrong, those who object to gestation crates but otherwise think meat or pork consumption is fine would not support or donate to the campaign.

To put this in simple terms: if Mary consumes meat but agrees that the gestation crate is cruel, she is going to donate to a campaign that she understands as saying that consuming animal products other than crated pork is morally better than consuming crated pork and that she is behaving more morally than people who consume crated pork. She is not going to support and donate to a campaign that says that what she is doing is no better morally than what those who consume crated pork are doing. As we can easily see, this situation results in promoting the idea that Mary's animal exploitation is morally acceptable.

An SIC against foie gras *must* promote the idea that eating a piece of steak, chicken, or fish, or pâté from the liver of a goose that has not been force fed is what people *ought* to do. If the campaign even suggested that people should stop eating all animal products or even just all meat, those who think that force feeding geese is wrong but that eating animal products is otherwise fine would not support—or donate to—the campaign. An SIC against fur must promote the idea that people ought to wear wool or leather instead of fur. If the anti-fur campaign even suggested that it was also immoral to wear wool or leather, those who think that it is tragic that seal cubs are clubbed or foxes are caught in leg hold traps but who wear wool and leather would not support or donate to the campaign. A campaign against the gestation crate *cannot* be understood to be promoting the eating of no pork, no meat, or no animal products, or it would fail to create a coalition because those who eat pork or other animal products would not support it.

All of these regulatory campaigns *must* engage in the pretense that the targeted activity or product is morally distinguishable from the activities or products that are not the subject of the regulatory campaign and that the latter are morally desirable alternatives. If those who are continuing to participate in animal exploitation are not told that their exploitation makes them "compassionate" people, they will not support the regulatory campaign. People must be made to feel comfortable and they are made to feel comfortable by an insidious pretense that the target of the campaign is immoral and their own conduct is not immoral, or is so much less immoral.

So, in effect, the coalitions for welfare reform and SICs all have one thing in common: they involve a broad spectrum of people who "care" about animals promoting exploitation that is supposedly more "humane," or promoting animal products or uses that are not the target of the welfare reform campaign or SIC.

A particularly pernicious effect of coalitions is that they render the moral imperative of veganism, which we will explore in greater detail when we come to *Principle Three,* as meaningless. By bringing together nonvegans and vegans (that is, vegans who support welfare and SICs) in order to form a group of people with a common goal, a coalition creates the false notion among its members and among the public that there is no moral difference between someone who deliberately exploits animals by being nonvegan and someone who does not do so by being vegan. Coalitions portray the act of not eating, wearing, and using animals as irrelevant or negligible to doing justice to animals. This, in effect, prevents veganism from being viewed as a moral requirement.

Is it possible for these campaigns to *not* promote animal exploitation? No. The *only* way that these campaigns can build coalitions is by promoting animal exploitation. Could welfarists reformulate these campaigns and promote welfare reform with a campaign that explicitly said, "We are promoting larger cages for laying hens but we oppose all animal exploitation however 'humane,' and we regard veganism as a moral imperative yet are seeking larger cages for chickens as an interim measure while we move toward the abolition of all animal exploitation"? Could they promote a single-issue campaign that explicitly said, "We regard all animal 'foods' as equally unjust and violative of animal rights, and we regard veganism as a moral baseline but we are targeting foie gras now and, as soon as we prevail, we will move on to other animal foods"? Sure, those are campaigns that could be promoted. But the *only* people who would support—*donate*—to such campaigns would be those who embraced animal rights. Such campaigns would have a great deal more moral integrity but they would be completely ineffective from a fundraising point of view. And that is precisely why no animal advocacy group has ever promoted those campaigns.

Third, welfare reform campaigns and SICs result in making "animal advocates" partners of institutional exploiters.

Given that these campaigns are all promoted by large animal advocacy organizations, the message is loud and clear: these organizations are putting a very clear stamp of approval on animal exploitation. In effect, animal advocates become at least implicit partners with the producers of the more "humane" products. These partnerships occur whenever these groups promote a reform campaign or SIC. However, in recent years, the outright promotion of animal exploitation through welfarist campaigns and SICs has become even more apparent as the result of explicit partnerships that are developing between animal advocates and institutional exploiters. These partnerships involve the former promoting the supposedly "happy" animal products marketed by the latter.

Although there have been instances of this going back to the 1990s, matters changed significantly in 2005 when Whole Foods Market, Inc., a chain of high-end supermarkets, announced that it wanted to develop a set of standards called "Animal Compassionate" standards, which would supposedly result in "higher-welfare" animal products. In January 2005, Peter Singer, author of *Animal Liberation* and widely regarded as the "father of the animal rights movement," sent a public letter to Whole Foods CEO John Mackey on behalf of the "undersigned animal welfare, animal protection and animal rights organizations," expressing "appreciation and support" for the "pioneering initiative being taken by Whole Foods" in developing these supposedly higher-welfare standards.[6] The groups that appeared as endorsing the letter included PETA, HSUS, Farm Sanctuary, Compassion Over Killing, Mercy for Animals, Vegan Outreach, and Viva! USA. Whole Foods publicized the letter. According to Mackey, PETA, Farm Sanctuary, Viva! USA, and other groups became "stakeholders" in the Whole Foods "happy exploitation" program and worked with Whole Foods to help develop supposedly "humane" methods of exploitation.[7]

---

[6] The letter from Singer and various animal advocacy groups expressing support for Whole Foods is available at: http://www.abolitionistapproach.com/wp-content/uploads/2013/05/support1.jpg

[7] The recording of Mackey's comments is available at: http://www.abolitionistapproach.com/?attachment_id=12936

Whole Foods collaborates with the Global Animal Partnership (GAP) and uses its 5-Step Animal Welfare Rating Program that allows consumers to choose what level of animal suffering they wish to purchase.[8] Animal welfare groups, including HSUS and CIWF, have representatives on the GAP board.[9] GAP works with Farm Forward, an organization that seeks "to align the needs of corporations for efficiency and profitability with production methods that foster sustainability and animal welfare."[10] Farm Forward works with PETA on its welfare reform campaigns, and has John Mackey on its board. PETA gave Whole Foods an Award for being the "Best Animal-Friendly Retailer."[11]

And the Whole Foods "happy exploitation" program is not the only one out there that is promoted by animal advocates. There are other similar schemes. For example, Humane Farm Animal Care, with its partners HSUS, the American Society for the Prevention of Cruelty to Animals, the World Society for the Protection of Animals, and others, promotes the "Certified Humane" label that seeks to increase the demand for a supposedly kinder and more responsible farm animal practices.[12] The Humane Society International, an arm of HSUS, has launched the "Humane Choice" label.[13] The RSPCA in Britain has the Freedom Food Label, which started in the 1990s.[14] CIWF gives almost 20 different Good Farm Animal Welfare Awards to recognize market leading food companies for their current policies or commitments that result in supposedly positive impacts on farm animal welfare across their supply chains.[15]

These are just a few of the various programs that animal welfare groups have adopted. There are other labeling programs and instances of various animal organizations explicitly embracing partnerships with institutional exploiters. But labeling programs are just one manifestation of the efforts

---

[8] http://www.wholefoodsmarket.com/mission-values/animal-welfare/collaboration-global-animal-partnership

[9] http://www.globalanimalpartnership.org/about/team

[10] https://farmforward.com/consulting-services

[11] http://www.abolitionistapproach.com/wp-content/uploads/2013/07/Picture1.jpg

[12] http://certifiedhumane.org/

[13] http://www.humanechoice.com.au/

[14] https://www.rspcaassured.org.uk/

[15] http://www.ciwf.org.uk/our-impact/food-business-programme/good-farm-animal-welfare-awards

and activities of modern "animal advocacy" groups that are explicitly intended to promote the idea of "happy exploitation." HSUS has a pig farmer, Joe Maxwell, who personally profits from the slaughter of 50,000 pigs per year, as Political Director of its Legislative Fund. Maxwell was formerly a Vice President of HSUS. And we are discussing here only a small fraction of many instances where supposed animal advocates have become active partners with industry. What all of these programs have in common is that supposed "animal advocates" are working with institutional exploiters to actively promote the consumption of animal products.

Elizabeth Heyrick, a nineteenth-century British campaigner against human slavery, argued that "gradual emancipation" allowed slave owners to transform themselves into moral champions by supporting "better" forms of slavery.[16] That is exactly what has happened with the modern "animal movement." People like Whole Foods CEO Mackey and "humane" pig farmers have become the new heroes.

Some animal welfare groups take the position that they oppose all exploitation and want ultimately to see the abolition of all animal use. Some animal groups just talk about the reduction of suffering and reduction of the numbers of animals used. But it really does not matter. Even if an animal organization claims to want abolition in a distant and nebulous future, their endorsement of welfare reforms and SICs as a means to that end effectively and often explicitly promotes the continued exploitation of nonhumans as things, albeit in a supposedly more "humane" way. That is no different from a peace organization saying that it values peace as the goal but promotes war as a morally good means to that end.

Welfarists often respond that they don't promote animal exploitation in promoting welfare reforms or SICs. But that is transparently false. When animal advocates call on industry to phase out the gestation crate in favor of a more "compassionate" alternative, or characterize cage-free eggs as the "responsible choice," or target fur as morally odious, those advocates are promoting "crate-free" pork, "cage-free" eggs, and leather or wool as normatively good things—as products that "compassionate" consumers *ought* to buy. That promotion is implicit in all reform campaigns and SICs and

---

[16]Elizabeth Coltman Heyrick, *Immediate, Not Gradual Abolition: or, An Inquiry into the Shortest, Safest, and Most Effectual Means of Getting Rid of West Indian Slavery* (1838), available at https://goo.gl/4iFsuw

it is explicit in the more recent campaigns in which animal advocates are forming partnerships with institutional exploiters. It is beyond ludicrous to say that when Peter Singer, joined by all of the large animal groups, expresses "appreciation and support" for the "pioneering" Whole Foods program of "compassionate" exploitation, they are not promoting the exploitation of animals. When PETA's Ingrid Newkirk says of Bell & Evans, a chicken producer, "Bell & Evans shows that animal welfare and good business can go hand in hand . . . and by listening to consumers' wishes, Bell & Evans has set a new standard for the chicken-supply industry,"[17] it is beyond ludicrous to say that Newkirk is not promoting the consumption of "happy" chicken. When HSUS employs a pig farmer as Political Director, it is beyond ludicrous to deny that HSUS is promoting the consumption of "happy" pork. And when HSUS actually sponsors events at which the corpses of "happy" animals are served,[18] it is impossible to deny that HSUS is promoting animal exploitation.

Welfarists also claim that even though they promote welfare reforms and SICs, they also take the position that "the best way you can help animals is simply to stop eating them" and so they are not promoting exploitation. Again, their claim is ludicrous. If someone promotes "humane" rape but adds that "the best way to respect the bodily integrity of women is not to rape them at all," that does not mean that the person is not promoting "humane" rape. The addition does not say that "humane" rape is wrong; the additional language does not in any way negate the promotion of "humane" rape as something normatively desirable. Indeed, what is communicated is that "humane" rape is good but that no rape is better. And to say that "humane" rape is good is, by definition, to promote it as a normative matter. It does not establish not committing rape as the moral baseline and as a moral imperative.

Fourth, welfare reform campaigns and SICs are speciesist.

If animal use is wrong—if animals have a right not to be used—then we should not promote "humane" or "happy" use any more than we should

---

[17] http://www.bellandevans.com/content/what-others-are-saying
[18] http://denver.thedrinknation.com/articles/read/13279-Sip-Sup-and-Move-Your-Feet-at-Hoofin-It-Aug-17-20

advocate the "humane" or "happy" violation of the fundamental rights of humans. The fact that we advocate "humane" animal exploitation where we would not do the same if humans were involved means that these regulatory campaigns are speciesist.

In order to see this, consider the violation of a fundamental human right. Slavery, rape, and torture all involve violations of fundamental human rights; they are all activities that should not happen *at all*. They all involve situations in which persons are treated as things; they are used as resources for others. Would anyone think it acceptable to campaign for "humane" slavery, "humane" rape, or "humane" torture? No, of course not. Although everyone condemns slavery, it still exists in many places in the world. Indeed, there are an estimated 27 million people enslaved at the present time—the highest number in human history. Does anyone propose that, rather than abolishing slavery, we should limit the number of times a slave owner can beat a slave? No, of course not. Several years ago, it was suggested that the United States develop rules to regulate the torture of those who were thought to have knowledge or information about terrorism and the idea of regulated torture was widely rejected.

To propose the regulation of the violation of a fundamental right is to accept the moral legitimacy of the violation of that fundamental right. To propose "humane" slavery, or "humane" rape, or "humane" torture is to accept that such activity is not ruled out as absolutely wrong and that it is merely a matter of *how* we do it. Violations of fundamental rights, including the right not to be used as property, involve excluding people altogether from the moral community and treating them as things that have no inherent value and whose value is only instrumental, whether to the slave owner, the rapist, or the torturer. To restore the status of the victim to that of being a moral person requires that we abolish their use as a thing, not that we make their use as a thing more "humane." The morality of slavery, rape, or torture does not depend on how "humanely" we treat slaves or victims of rape or torture; we regard all of these activities as inherently immoral precisely because they remove victims entirely from the moral community. These activities are inherently unjust; there is no right way to do them.

Consider that in the nineteenth century there was a significant movement in Britain to abolish vivisection. The death knell of that movement was the passage of legislation that purported to regulate vivisection and make it "humane." Indeed, such legislation normalized vivisection and accepted it as a morally legitimate activity. So a campaign to regulate vivisection ended up increasing public acceptance of vivisection.

If humans and nonhumans are equal for purposes of having a fundamental right not to be used as things, and if we would not support campaigns to make violations of fundamental human rights more "humane," then we should not treat the violation of the fundamental rights of nonhumans in a different way because of species. *To do otherwise involves speciesism.*

It is certainly better to cause less harm than more. That is not only common sense; it is enshrined in the law. If X rapes Y and also tortures Y, X will be more harshly punished than if he raped Y but did not torture Y. But if X raped Y but did not torture Y, no one would say that X did something morally good or that X was a "compassionate" rapist. But that is *exactly* what welfare reform campaigns do: they promote the idea that causing supposedly less harm makes animal use morally good and compassionate, or, at the very least, something that is not morally wrong and morally objectionable.

SICs are speciesist in a particular way in that they create a hierarchy in which certain animals are favored over other animals. In certain respects, welfare campaigns do this as well, but SICs do it more clearly. For example, campaigns that concern nonhuman great apes, dolphins and other marine mammals, and elephants all focus on how similar these animals are cognitively and emotionally (and, in the case of nonhuman great apes, genetically) to humans. This approach results in the creation of a hierarchy that privileges certain animals and falsely portrays them as being more worthy of consideration and protection. Although it is true that certain nonhumans are more similar to humans, linking that similarity with moral value assumes that humanlike cognition is more valuable than mere sentience, a position rejected by the Abolitionist Approach and that we will explore in greater detail when we get to *Principle Four.*

In other cases, the different treatment based on species is implicit. For example, consider one of the oldest SICs—the anti-fur campaign. What is the moral difference between fur and other animal clothing, such as wool or leather? That's easy to answer: there is none. Animals used for leather and wool are no less worthy morally than are animals used for making fur garments or trim. But the anti-fur campaign conveys the notion that animals exploited to make fur are somehow more morally valuable than the animals used to make leather or wool clothing. Campaigns against the eating of dogs and cats in Asian countries convey the idea that it is morally more odious to consume dogs and cats than it is to consume cows, pigs, chickens, or fish. A campaign against foie gras is based on the idea that foie gras is different from, and worse than, other meats. The Meatless Monday campaign conveys the idea that animals exploited for meat matter more than animals who are exploited for dairy or eggs.

In response to the abolitionist position that it is speciesist to promote more "humane" animal exploitation when we would not support "humane" slavery, "humane" rape, or "humane" violations of other fundamental human rights, welfarists claim that we *do* support more "humane" violations of fundamental human rights.

The usual example they give is that of Amnesty International. Amnesty International opposes imprisonment for political reasons and they work to get those political prisoners released. But if they cannot get the prisoners released, they will oppose any torture of those prisoners. Welfarists liken their efforts to those of Amnesty International, claiming that they can't get the animals out of the oppressive conditions but they can fight to stop the torture.

The analogy fails in several ways.

All animal exploitation involves subjecting animals to treatment which would, were humans involved, constitute torture. That is, the entire process of raising animals for food, for instance, involves suffering, fear, and distress from the moment of birth to the moment of death. The welfarists arbitrarily pick practices that are already "low-hanging fruit" because they are economically inefficient and they fail to recognize that the *entire* process of animal exploitation involves torture. Welfarists are not analogous to Amnesty International, which objects to imprisonment on political grounds and, if release cannot be secured, demands that prisoners not be tortured. Welfarists are working with industry to *reform* torture; Amnesty International does not do that. When welfarists promote an "enriched" cage or a "cage-free" barn for laying hens, they are not demanding that torture end; they are, instead, promoting alternatives that also result in the torture of the birds. The idea that an "enriched" cage or a "cage-free" barn does not involve torture could only be advanced by someone who knew nothing about these alternatives to conventional battery cages. What animal welfarists do would be analogous to Amnesty International promoting the position that when prisoners receive electrical shocks, the shocks should be administered for no longer than three hours without a one minute break. And Amnesty International does not support such positions because torture involves violating a fundamental human right and should not occur *at all.*

Moreover, as we saw above, welfare campaigns necessarily promote animal exploitation because they portray the reformed situation as "compassionate" or otherwise describe it in positive normative terms, which is the only way that coalitions can be formed around these reform campaigns. Although this is true of *all* welfarist campaigns, it is particularly true of the modern welfarist approach where animal groups have entered into explicit partnerships with institutional exploiters and publicly express their "appreciation and support" for supposedly "humane" reforms upon which they put a stamp of approval and give awards and accolades to institutional exploiters. Amnesty International does not give awards to dictators who promise to whip their political prisoners nine times a week rather than ten.

Welfarists also claim that Amnesty International opposes the death penalty but proposes more "humane" methods of execution. That is simply false. Amnesty condemns the death penalty irrespective of method.[19]

Another example relied on by welfarists is civil rights reforms. They argue that animal welfare reforms are similar to civil rights reforms and that, since we supported the latter, we ought to support the former. But, again, the analogy does not hold. Civil rights reforms occur in the context where we are talking about those who are regarded as persons and not things, as are slaves, torture victims, rape victims, or other humans whose fundamental rights are being violated. The question presented by a civil rights reform campaign is whether the reform is necessary to assure equal treatment of equal interests in order to resolve competing claims of persons. To say that the Civil Rights Act of 1954 (a U.S. law that outlawed racial segregation in theaters, restaurants, and hotels and rejected the claims of property owners that they were free to exclude whom they wished from their property) is analogous to a reform of slavery that prohibits a slave owner from beating his slaves more than ten times a week or a reform that requires a one-minute break in the torture sessions of political prisoners, is absurd. We could not

---

[19] https://www.amnesty.org/en/what-we-do/death-penalty/;
http://www.amnesty.org.au/adp/comments/36773

reform our way out of slavery. The institution of slavery had to be abolished before civil rights initiatives could provide greater equality to people who were no longer considered to be property.

Welfarists also note that we pursue SICs in the human context. For example, we may have a campaign that targets genocide in Somalia but does not address genocide in Burundi or any other country. Welfarists claim that if SICs are problematic in the animal context and that if animal advocates should not pursue them, then it follows that SICs are similarly problematic in the human context and human rights advocates ought not to pursue them either.

Once again, welfarists do not recognize that there are important differences that make SICs in the human context relevantly different. When we oppose genocide in Somalia, we are not making any statement that genocide in Burundi or in other places is in any way more morally acceptable, or that the genocide in Burundi is the sort of genocide that Somalia ought to adopt. Our starting position is that genocide as an activity is morally wrong. So a campaign against genocide in one country *cannot* be understood as giving a green light to genocide in another country. But in the animal context, the starting point is that animal exploitation is morally acceptable (at least as long as it is "humane"), so a campaign against foie gras can *only* be understood as maintaining that foie gras is morally worse than other animal foods, which, by implication, are morally acceptable. A campaign against fur can *only* be understood as giving a green light to wool or leather.

A campaign against genocide in Somalia does not require the participation of people who support genocide in another country. On the contrary. Those opposing genocide in Somalia are not likely to want to include in their coalition anyone who supports genocide anywhere. SICs that involve animal uses or products *require* the participation of those who actively support and participate in relevantly indistinguishable forms of animal exploitation.

Fifth, SICs promote discrimination against humans.

By creating a coalition of people—many of whom engage in animal exploitation, but who are united in promoting the idea that *some* animal products or uses are morally more odious than other products and uses—SICs not only promote the supposedly more moral products and uses, but they create an "us/them" dichotomy that arbitrarily demonizes people who consume the targeted product or engage in the targeted use. Again, the only way that members of the SIC coalition can be made to feel comfortable is by fostering the pretense that they are different from, and "better" than, the "bad" people who are engaging in the activity that is the target of the campaign. So women who wear fur are portrayed as terrible human beings and as morally different from those who wear leather or wool. Asians who eat dogs, cats, or whales, or who kill dolphins—or hunters who kill lions, giraffes, or other animals—are depicted as morally inferior to those who consume cows, pigs, chickens, and fish.

The reality, however, is that all those who violate the fundamental right of nonhuman animals not to be used as resources and who treat nonhuman animals as things, are, from a moral perspective, the same. So attacking a woman wearing fur as a terrible person ignores the fact that she is morally no different from those who wear leather or wool, or who consume meat, dairy, or eggs, or who otherwise use animals as things. The Asians who consume dogs, cats, or whales are no different from the Americans, British, Germans, or French who consume pork, beef, chicken, fish, etc. The vivisector who does experiments involving primates is morally no different from the vivisector who uses rats, and neither vivisector is different from the person who wears wool or leather, or who eats meat, dairy, or eggs.

This demonization is bad enough in itself for the obvious reason that it is arbitrary and irrational, but, as is often the case, the people who end up being characterized as morally odious and as inferior to others are women, people of color, other minorities, or those from foreign nations. These campaigns frequently involve racism and sexism, as well as xenophobia and ethnocentrism.

Consider the anti-fur campaign. The choice of fur as a target over leather or wool is itself problematic given that fur is a garment that has traditionally been worn by women and is part of what patriarchal culture dictates as fashion. Interestingly, leather and wool have never been the targets of any sustained campaigns. Anti-fur campaigns have literally demonized women who wear fur and have created the impression that people—almost always women—who wear fur are more morally odious than everyone else. In one of the most well-known images associated with the anti-fur movement, a woman, seen only from the waist down, wearing black stockings and high heels, is dragging a fur coat leaving a trail of blood. The caption reads, "It takes 40 dumb animals to make a fur coat. But only one to wear it." Animal advocates who target fur often engage in aggressive ways in public toward women who wear fur. If one ever wants to hear a litany of misogynistic invectives, one need only go to an anti-fur protest and hear the abusive comments made—often by people wearing leather or wool—to women passing by who are wearing fur.

Animal advocates have targeted a Jewish ritual called Kapparot or Kaporos.[20] This event occurs on the eve of Yom Kippur and involves swinging a chicken over one's head during which one symbolically transfers one's sins to the chicken, who is then killed by having her throat slit. What happens to the chickens used in this ritual is no different from what happens in any slaughterhouse. But advocates in North America and Europe, as well as in Australia, target kosher slaughter and halal slaughter, both of which involve the exsanguination of an animal who is not stunned. In all of these cases, the use of the animal in the ritual context is explicitly or implicitly characterized as worse than in the non-ritual context. In all of these cases, there are people who eat meat and other animal products opposing the use of animals in the ritual context. In all of these cases, animal advocates explicitly promote the idea that a solution to the problem is to support only the consumption of animals who have been stunned. For example, one group in Britain, Viva!, stated in connection with a campaign against halal slaughter, "Consumers can do their bit by boycotting places that persist in selling meat from unstunned animals."[21] Such a statement explicitly promotes the consumption of meat from stunned animals as well as reinforces the idea that Muslims or Jews who keep kosher are morally more odious than everyone else. There can be no doubt that such campaigns foster anti-Semitism and Islamophobia. Indeed, in connection with the Kapparot campaign, one of the authors of this book contacted those who are promoting that campaign and asked that the campaign include a statement that anyone who opposed the Kapparot ritual should understand that the practitioners of the ritual are no different from anyone who consumes chicken (or any other animal products). The request was declined.

---

[20] http://www.endchickensaskaporos.com
[21] http://www.dailymail.co.uk/news/article-1313303

Other uses of animals in ritual contexts involve the killing of animals in connection with Santería and similar religions, which are religions of Caribbean origin that developed in the Spanish Empire among slaves from West Africa. Animal advocates have targeted these uses although there is no morally coherent distinction between the killing of animals in Santería and the killing of animals in any other context.

When we discuss *Principle Five* we will explore in further detail why the Abolitionist Approach opposes racism, sexism, heterosexism, and all other forms of human discrimination, in addition to speciesism.

Sixth, welfare reforms and SICs are ineffective.

Abolitionists would still object to regulation even if it were effective. To understand why, think about the issue in the human context. If we think that human slavery is unjust, we should promote the abolition of human slavery and not campaign for measures to regulate slavery, even if we think that regulation might be effective. But in the context of animal exploitation, regulation is *not* effective. We have been regulating animal exploitation for about 200 years now, and we are exploiting more animals in more horrific ways than at any point in human history. We will look at welfare reforms and SICs separately. We will also examine the argument that welfarists have recently begun to raise and promote: that "science" shows that welfare reform is "effective."

Animal Welfare Reforms

Animal welfare reforms are not effective because they *cannot* be effective; the property status of animals imposes structural limitations on welfare reform. Because animals are property, animal welfare standards will always be low. As we saw in our discussion of *Principle One,* animals, as property, not only have no rights, but humans have property rights in animals.

It costs money to protect animal interests and that severely limits the level of protection we will provide. Moreover, how do we determine which interests ought to be protected when the overwhelming portion of our use of animals—in fact, just about all of it—cannot be plausibly characterized as "necessary" in any way?

The greatest number of animals we use is for food. We kill approximately

60 billion land animals per year for food and we kill an estimated one trillion sea animals. What is the justification for all of that suffering and death? There is no need, no compulsion, to eat animals for reasons of human health. Indeed, just about every governmental organization, professional organization, and research institution has conceded that a diet containing no animal foods is not only satisfactory for health purposes but is probably more healthy. The only justification we have for inflicting suffering and death on the staggering number of animals we use for food is that they taste good. The same point holds true for the animals we use for clothing. There is no reason beyond fashion sense to justify our use of wool, leather, fur, etc. And, by definition, there is no necessity for using nonhumans in entertainment contexts, such as sport hunting, circuses, rodeos, bullfights, etc.

Given that just about all of the suffering that we impose on animals is not necessary, how are we to make sense of the moral and legal principle that we should not impose "unnecessary" suffering on animals? How do we determine the level of protection that we ought to give to animals?

The answer is clear: we will protect animal interests when it is beneficial for us to do so. We will generally prohibit forms of treatment that do not provide any sort of economic benefit and that, on the contrary, decrease the value of animal property. We will require only that level of protection for animal interests that is required to exploit the animal in an economically efficient way. Because "necessary" suffering is linked to what is required to facilitate animal use, the standard for "humane" treatment is, not surprisingly, largely determined by what is regarded as customary in the particular industry of exploitation. And if we want to know what is needed to use animals for a particular purpose, the best people to consult are those who use them for that purpose because we assume that it would be irrational for them to impose gratuitous harm (and resulting economic damage) on their property. This is exactly how the law works. As a result, anticruelty laws often explicitly exempt the "normal" or "regular" practices of a particular institutionalized animal use, such as animal agriculture. And even when these statutes do not contain an explicit exemption, courts have interpreted anticruelty laws to require only that treatment that is normal or customary in the industry.

The prohibition on imposing "unnecessary" suffering is, for the most part, a prohibition only on imposing *gratuitous* suffering that a rational property owner with full information would not impose in the first place. The law will generally not impose an obligation on animal owners to do anything that will not be economically beneficial to the process of producing animal products. At least insofar as animal welfare laws are concerned, animal welfare is, for the most part, about ensuring that animal use is economically efficient.

For example, consider the U.S. Humane Slaughter Act, enacted originally in 1958, which requires that larger animals slaughtered for food be stunned and not be conscious when they are shackled, hoisted, and taken to the killing floor. This law protects the interests that animals have at the moment of slaughter, but it is clear that the paramount concerns that motivated the legislation were economic: large animals who are conscious and hanging upside down and thrashing as they are slaughtered will cause injuries to slaughterhouse workers and will incur expensive carcass damage. Therefore, stunning large animals makes good economic sense.

Of course, these animals have many other interests throughout their lives, including an interest in avoiding pain and suffering at times other than at the moment of slaughter, and these other interests are not protected because it is not economically effective to do so. Interestingly, the Humane Slaughter Act has not been interpreted to apply to smaller animals, including birds, who account for most of the animals slaughtered for food in the United States. The reason for this exclusion is that given the number of birds slaughtered, and their relatively smaller size and lesser value, it has not been considered economically efficient to protect the interests of chickens in the same way as the interests of cows. But as we will see below, welfarists are campaigning for more "humane" poultry slaughter precisely on the basis that recent studies in agricultural economics indicate that more "humane" slaughter would be economically beneficial to the producers of animal products.

Mindful of the limitations of animal welfare laws, many animal welfare organizations have sought to get industry to voluntarily adopt welfare reforms that are supposedly more progressive than what has been protected by animal welfare laws thus far. But even these measures reflect the reality that animal welfare regulation is primarily about economically efficient animal exploitation. If we look at the campaigns that are promoted by the large animal welfare groups, we see that, for the most part, these campaigns identify economically vulnerable industry practices and they propose solutions that increase production efficiency. Let's focus on just three of many examples: persuading fast-food restaurants to get their meat suppliers to implement standards set by agricultural scientist Temple Grandin; the use of controlled-atmosphere killing (CAK)—or, simply put, gassing—to kill poultry; and the elimination of the gestation crate used to confine pregnant and newly delivered sows.

(1) Temple Grandin is an internationally renowned agricultural scientist who claims that her autism gives her a special insight into the thinking of animals. Grandin designs slaughterhouses that are supposedly informed by her autistic insight, and she advises the livestock industry about animal behavior and animal handling. She is praised by Peter Singer and HSUS, and PETA gave her an award proclaiming her to be a "visionary" in her promotion of animal welfare reform. PETA persuaded various fast-food chains to set and enforce supposedly "higher" standards for slaughterhouses from which they obtained meat; and these standards were formulated by Grandin, who focuses explicitly on economic concerns. According to Grandin, "Once livestock—cattle, pigs and sheep—arrive at packing plants, proper handling procedures are not only important for the animal's well-being, they can also mean the difference between profit and loss. Research clearly demonstrates that many meat quality benefits can be obtained with careful, quiet animal handling."[22] She adds, "Gentle handling in well-designed facilities will minimize stress levels, improve efficiency and maintain good meat quality."[23]

(2) PETA argues[24] that CAK is economically more advantageous than the present electric stunning method because CAK "increases product quality and yield;" decreases carcass contamination and the damage to meat from the scalding that occurs in the defeathering process; increases the "shelf-life of meat;" results in "'more tender breast meat;'" and "lowers labor costs" by reducing the need for certain inspections, reducing accidents, and lowering employee turnover. CAK provides "other economic benefits" to the poultry industry by allowing producers to save money on energy costs and water usage. PETA concludes, "Considering the improvements in carcass quality, product yield, and labor costs that come with controlled-atmosphere killing, it is no surprise that a return on investment (ROI) in CAK can be reached

---

[22] http://www.grandin.com/RecAnimalHandlingGuidelines.html

[23] http://www.grandin.com/meat/meat.html

[24] http://www.peta.org/features/case-controlled-atmosphere-killing (click on "CAK Economic Analysis"). HSUS has a similar economic analysis of CAK. See http://www.abolitionistapproach.com/media/links/p31/hsus-report-practices.pdf

in as little as one year."

(3) In its campaign to promote alternatives to the gestation crate to confine breeding pigs, HSUS cites an Iowa State University study which found that "[r]eproductive performance can be maintained or enhanced in well-managed group housing systems . . . without increasing labor." Overall, the study concluded that "[g]roup housing . . . resulted in a weaned pig cost that was 11 percent less than the cost of a weaned pig from the individual stall confinement system."[25]

These sorts of campaigns indicate quite clearly that animal advocates who promote welfare reforms may say that these reforms are about moving animals away from the property paradigm but, contrary to any such claim, these reforms simply make the exploitation of animal property more efficient and further enmesh animals in the property paradigm.

Moreover, even in cases where animal welfare reform goes beyond making animal exploitation more efficient and results in more expensive production costs, any increase in price will not move animals away from being property and toward being moral persons. So even if cage-free eggs or free-range eggs are moderately more expensive to produce, or even if the "happy" meat and other animal products sold by Whole Foods or artisan producers cost more money, that will not mean that animals stop being property to the extent of that increase. They just become more expensive property. They remain things, just as a Porsche, although more expensive than a Ford, is still a thing. The fact that consumers may be willing to pay more for these artisan products does not mean that they reject the idea that animals should be used as property. If they did reject that view, they would not be consuming animals at all. And there is *no* reason to believe that the presence of artisan or "higher" welfare products has any cultural impact in terms of shifting views about the status of animals as resources.

To the extent that welfarists maintain that welfare reforms that result in price increases reduce demand for animal products, they miss four points:

First, they ignore that, in just about all cases, consumers are not forced to purchase the "higher" welfare product. That is, a consumer in Britain who does not want to pay extra for the supposedly more "humanely" raised British pork can buy "lower" welfare pork from France, Germany, or other

---

[25] http://www.humanesociety.org/issues/confinement_farm/facts/gestation_crates.html

E.U. countries.

Second, even in those rare situations in which consumers are forced to buy the "higher" welfare product, as they are in the E.U. as the result of a Community-wide rule requiring that laying hens be confined in "enriched" cages rather than in conventional cages, the demand for most basic animal products is what economists call *inelastic;* that is, the demand is not very sensitive to price increases. So, if necessary, people will go to fewer movies or will put off purchasing a new computer rather than buy fewer eggs even if they become moderately more expensive.

If there are going to be significant changes in animal treatment, these changes will occur only if there is a widespread demand for such products and a willingness both to pay the resulting much higher costs that significant change would entail and to keep lower-welfare products out of the market.

Third, even if an animal product becomes more expensive to the point where demand starts to be affected, consumers will not switch to a non-animal product; they will look for an alternative *animal* product. To put the matter another way, if beef becomes too expensive, consumers will buy more pork and chicken. They will not switch to tofu.

Fourth, the very best that welfare reform can do is to create a niche market where affluent consumers can buy supposedly more "humanely" produced animal products and feel better about continuing to consume animals. But the *most* "humanely" produced animal product still involves suffering, death, and injustice. It still involves treatment that, however "humane," would be objectionable were humans involved. Animal welfare, whether tied to standards that merely ensure efficient exploitation or whether tied to a standard that actually increases prices, will always be low and will always serve to make people feel better morally about exploiting animals.

As for the immediacy of helping animals, it is ludicrous to suggest that animal welfare reforms help animals "now." Almost all welfare reforms are phased in over periods of years and, in some cases, many years, if they are ever put into effect at all. And if they are put into effect, these reforms provide little, if any, protection for animal interests. They may result in slightly less torture, but to celebrate a bit less torture as "helping animals" is perverse. Imagine a situation in which a blowtorch is being applied to you for ten seconds. Would you think that reducing the application of the blowtorch to nine seconds should be characterized as "helping" you? We certainly would not.

Finally, it is important to realize that if animal advocates did not pursue welfare reform campaigns and instead promoted the abolition of animal use and veganism, institutional exploiters would make the same sorts of reforms in order to fend off the threat of a vegan movement by reassuring the public in an attempt to keep existing customers and encourage others to return. The main difference would be that animal advocates would not be acting as partners of institutional exploiters and encouraging the public to continue to consume and exploit animals in a supposedly more "compassionate" way.

And let us be crystal clear: the reforms that are promoted by welfarists do not result in significant increases in protection for animal interests. An egg from a "cage-free" hen and an egg from a conventionally caged hen both are eggs that involve suffering, death, and injustice. A slaughterhouse designed by Temple Grandin, praised by PETA, and a slaughterhouse not designed by Temple Grandin are both hideous places.

Single-Issue Campaigns

Welfarists claim that SICs, by focusing on particular uses, can, after enough SICs, add up to a challenge to animal use. So if we have a successful anti-fur campaign and eradicate fur, we can move on to leather and then to wool. If we have a successful anti-foie gras campaign and people stop eating foie gras, we can move on to other meat. And when we have had successful SICs aimed at all different sorts of meat, we can move on to dairy and then to eggs.

But this scenario is nothing but a welfarist fantasy. Consider the two longest-running SICs: the anti-fur campaign and the anti-vivisection campaign. The anti-fur campaign has been going on for 40 years now and the fur industry is stronger than ever. The anti-vivisection movement has been in existence for the better part of 200 years and more animals are being used in vivisection than ever before. SICs operate by arbitrarily distinguishing one product or use from other products or uses and by characterizing the target product or use as morally worse than the others. They build coalitions based on the common rejection of the target by coalition members who embrace other forms of exploitation that are morally indistinguishable from the target. To say that, once the targeted product or use has been abolished, a new coalition will be formed to attack another product or use that was formerly characterized as morally acceptable is not a coherent or realistic strategy. And it is not one calculated to convey to the public clarity and integrity in the position of the animal advocacy movement.

Welfarists sometimes defend SICSs by saying that SICs get people thinking about animal issues by focusing them on one thing, such as fur, and that welfarists can then broaden the focus to other issues. Such a position amounts to saying that animal advocates have campaigns that promote supposedly more "humane" exploitation and then turn around and tell people that what they have previously been told is "humane" is not. It is easy to see the moral and practical problems with such an approach, including that this makes animal advocates appear as completely dishonest. If someone campaigns against fur only to be told by the people who encouraged their support and donations, "Hey, by the way, we did not bother to tell you that wool and leather are actually no better than fur," they are not likely to think very highly of this "bait and switch" approach. Moreover, the anti-fur campaign has been going for decades now and welfarists have not convinced people about fur, let alone wool, leather, silk, or the use of animals for food, entertainment, etc.

SICs also certainly don't help any animals "now." For the most part, SICs encourage people to consume *other* animal products or engage in *other* forms of animal exploitation. If people stop eating foie gras, they may help the geese used to make foie gras but they will not help the cows, pigs, chickens, and fish that people consume when they don't consume foie gras. When people stop wearing fur, they may help the animals who are used to make fur coats. They do not help the sheep, cows, and other animals used to make the products that people buy when they don't buy fur.

And What Does "Science" Say?

In 2009, several agricultural economists published a paper claiming that, although meat consumption is increasing, it did not increase quite as much as the authors thought it would have with respect to pigs and chickens. The authors noted that there was media attention to animal welfare issues during the relevant time period. They concluded that this media attention to animal welfare issues played a role in the lower-than-expected increase in consumption of pigs and chickens, although the reduction in increase was, in any event, "small."[26] In other words, consumption of meat is increasing but the increase was slightly less than what was expected and this small reduction in expected increase may have been due to media attention given to issues of animal welfare.

You do not have to be an expert in data analysis to see that any claim that this study shows that welfare reform campaigns are effective in some way (other than bringing in donations to corporate charities) is unfounded.

First and foremost, looking at *any* data about the consumption of animals and trying to link it with animal welfare campaigns is speculative at best. *Could* animal welfare campaigns also have played some role in the "small" reduction in expected increase in consumption? Sure, but so could the economy, weather, reports about the health and environmental consequences of meat consumption, efforts by grassroots advocates who promoted veganism and criticized welfare reform campaigns during the relevant time period, or many other things. It is interesting that the authors did *not* find the same "small" reduction in expected increase in the consumption of cows although many animal welfare campaigns during the relevant time period focused on cows. In any event, any claim by the authors of the study that welfare campaigns have a meaningful impact on the consumption of animals is not only unwarranted; it is irresponsible.

Second, those who reduced their consumption of pigs and chickens *for whatever reason* may have shifted to many of the other animal products as the authors only looked at cows, pigs, and poultry.

In short, this study showed that animal consumption is increasing, but

---

[26]The essay can be accessed and is discussed here: http://www.abolitionistapproach.com/science-weighs-in-animal-welfare-reform-is-useless

that it did not increase as much with respect to pigs and chickens; and that might have been due to animal welfare campaigns, but it might have had nothing to do with animal welfare campaigns. Any failure of demand increase may very well reflect a shift to fish, eggs, dairy products, and prepared meat foods.

In other words, this study showed *nothing* of relevance to the empirical question whether animal welfare reform campaigns are effective in reducing animal consumption. That did not, however, stop the welfarists from declaring, as did the late welfarist campaigner Norm Phelps, that "science" showed that welfare campaigns "cause people to buy significantly less meat."[27] Groups like Farm Sanctuary and Mercy for Animals characterize this study as showing that the welfare reform campaigns that these groups promote result in people eating less meat.

Any such claim is absurd and clearly so.

In our discussion of *Principle Three,* we will examine claims by the welfarists that "science" also shows we should promote nonveganism if we want people to go vegan and that, in any event, we will reduce animal suffering more if we promote reducing animal consumption than if we promote veganism. We will see that those claims are also unfounded.

---

[27] http://www.evana.org/index.php?id=63506

A Note on Goals and Strategies

Welfarists often claim that they are really "abolitionists" who agree that we should abolish animal use, but that they simply disagree on the "strategy" that we should use to achieve that end. If someone claims to be an abolitionist but supports welfare reform as a strategy or means to achieve abolition, they are using "abolition" in a fundamentally different way from the way in which we use that term. We use that term to identify a position that *excludes* regulation/welfare reform as being *inherently inconsistent* with abolition.

Think about it this way: Mary and John both claim to be peace advocates. Mary wants to achieve world peace as a goal and advocates nonviolent conflict resolution as a strategy or means to that end. John also claims to want to achieve world peace as a goal and advocates war as a means to the end of peace. (This second position pretty much describes American foreign policy, actually.) Both Mary and John claim to be peace advocates but John advocates a means—violence—that is *directly* contrary to, and *completely* inconsistent with, the claimed end of peace. John argues that war—the opposite of peace—is an acceptable strategy or means to the end of peace.

When looked at in this context, we can easily see the problem of promoting a strategy that is inconsistent with the end that the strategy supposedly seeks.

Animal advocates who support welfare reform often claim that they seek abolition as a goal; they claim to want to eliminate all animal use. But they advocate "happy" use as a strategy or means to the end of no use. As we will see when we discuss *Principle Three*, they advocate reducing meat, both as a normatively desirable thing to do and as a purported strategy or means to achieve veganism. This is similar to using war as a strategy or means to the end of nonviolence and peace.

We maintain that "abolitionist" is properly used only if the means are consistent with the end. As we will see in the next chapter, we advocate veganism on the individual level, and creative, nonviolent vegan education on the social level as the only strategy or means that is consistent with the abolition of animal exploitation. The end is no use and the means chosen to get to that end are no use on the individual level and education of no use on the social level.

Abolition, as we use that term, rules out welfare regulation. Abolition, as we use that term, rules out the position that "happy" use is an acceptable way to get to no use just as we regard war as a morally unacceptable way to achieve peace. We also think it is clear that just as war does not work to bring about a peaceful world and that violence begets more violence, promoting "happy" violence against animals will just result in people feeling more comfortable about violence against animals. The economic success of the "happy exploitation" industry and the proliferation of "happy exploitation" labels certainly suggest that is the case.

Where fundamental rights are involved, we can *never* promote a violation of those rights to achieve a nonviolation of those rights. We can see this where the fundamental rights of humans are involved. No one would advocate "gentle" racism as a strategy or means to achieve racial equality. No one would advocate "gentle" sexism as a strategy or means to achieve gender equality. No would advocate "gentle" rape as a strategy or means to achieve no rape. No one would advocate "gentle" pedophilia as a strategy or means to achieve no pedophilia.

But where animals are concerned, many so-called animal advocates think it is appropriate to promote a supposedly more "gentle" violation of the fundamental rights of animals to achieve animal rights. We maintain that such a position is not only counterproductive in practical terms but that we would also all agree it would be morally obscene in the human context. We reject the speciesism of the welfarist position.

Conclusion

The promotion of any animal use is completely inconsistent with the Abolitionist Approach, which maintains that nonhuman animals have a fundamental right not to be used as resources for humans—however "humanely" they may be treated. If animal use is wrong—if animals have a right not to be used—then we cannot advocate "humane" or "happy" use. To put the matter another way: less suffering is always better than more suffering but a social justice movement for animals should *never* be advocating that imposing less suffering is a morally acceptable or desirable thing to do.

Welfarists claim that animal use is not going to end "overnight" and that we need a program of incremental change—we need "baby steps." Abolitionists agree that exploitation is not going to end "overnight" and that we need an incremental strategy. The difference is that abolitionists reject welfare reform and SICs as incremental steps because they are not only ineffective, but also because they actually promote animal exploitation and so, to the extent that they represent "steps" of any sort, they represent big steps backward. The strategy proposed by the Abolitionist Approach will be discussed in the next section.

Focusing on "humane" treatment reinforces the idea that animals are things we can use as resources as long as we do so in a "humane" way. That may reinforce the idea that we have an obligation to use animals "humanely" but it does not reinforce or even suggest the idea that we ought not to use animals. In any event, if animals have the moral right not to be used as things, which abolitionists maintain, promoting supposedly "humane" exploitation is no more an option than is claiming to want peace but advocating war as a means to get to peace. The promotion of welfare reforms and SICs does *nothing* but reassure the public that "compassionate" exploitation is possible. It isn't.

Further Reading

Books

Gary L. Francione & Robert Garner, *The Animal Rights Debate: Abolition or Regulation?* (Columbia University Press 2010).

Gary L. Francione, *Animals as Persons: Essays in the Abolition of Animal Exploitation* (Columbia University Press 2008), 67-128.

Gary L. Francione, *Rain Without Thunder: The Ideology of the Animal Rights Movement* (Temple University Press 1996).

Gary L. Francione, *Animals, Property, and the Law* (Temple University Press 1995).

Essays

Gary L. Francione, "Animal Welfare and the Moral Value of Nonhuman Animals," *Law, Culture and the Humanities* 6 (1) 1-13 (2009).

Gary L. Francione, "Reflections on *Animals, Property, and the Law* and *Rain Without Thunder*," 70 *Law and Contemporary Problems* 9-57 (2007), and reprinted in Gary L. Francione, *Animals as Persons: Essays in the Abolition of Animal Exploitation* (Columbia University Press 2008), 67-128.

Blog Posts

"Welfare Reform Campaigns, Single-Issue Campaigns, and Animal Exploitation: Perfect Together," at
www.abolitionistapproach.com/welfare-reform-campaigns-single-issue-campaigns-and-animal-exploitation-perfect-together

"The Economics of Animal Welfare: Some Brief Comments," at
www.abolitionistapproach.com/economics-animal-welfare

"Animal Welfare Regulation, "Happy Exploitation," and Speciesism," at
www.abolitionistapproach.com/animal-welfare-regulation-happy-exploitation-and-speciesism

"The Four Problems of Animal Welfare: In a Nutshell," at www.abolitionistapproach.com/the-four-problems-of-animal-welfare-in-a-nutshell

Principle Three

Abolitionists maintain that veganism is a moral baseline and that creative, nonviolent vegan education must be the cornerstone of rational animal rights advocacy.

Summary

Abolitionists embrace the idea that there is veganism and there is animal exploitation: there is no third choice. To not be a vegan is to participate directly in animal exploitation. Abolitionists promote veganism as a moral baseline or a moral imperative and as the *only* rational response to the recognition that animals have moral value. If animals matter morally, then we cannot treat them as commodities and eat, wear, or use them. Just as someone who promoted the abolition of slavery could not own slaves, an abolitionist with respect to animal slavery cannot consume animal products. For an abolitionist, veganism is a fundamental matter of justice. As the Abolitionist Approach is a grassroots movement, advocating veganism as a fundamental principle of justice is not something that requires large, wealthy charities and "leaders." It is something that we all can do and must do as a grassroots movement. Each of us must be a leader.

Discussion

Veganism as a Moral Imperative

Abolitionists agree with welfarists that animal exploitation is not going to disappear "overnight" and that we need to take incremental steps—what welfarists call "baby steps"—to get to the goal of abolition. But abolitionists reject welfare reform campaigns and single-issue campaigns (SICs) as incremental steps because they are inconsistent with the idea that nonhuman animals are morally significant and have the right not to be used as resources for humans. Additionally, as a practical matter, these tactics do not work and, by their very nature, cannot lead to abolition.

Despite claims by welfarists that abolitionists have no practical plan for change, abolitionists have a very clear program for incremental change on both the individual and social levels: veganism and creative, nonviolent vegan advocacy and education. *Veganism means not eating, wearing, or otherwise using animals to the extent practicable.*

We should state at the outset that *no one* maintains that it's medically necessary to eat animal foods. Mainstream professional organizations, including the Academy of Nutrition and Dietetics, the American Diabetes Association, the American Heart Association, the British Dietetic Association, the British Nutritional Foundation, Dietician's Association of Australia, Dieticians of Canada, and the Heart and Stroke Foundation; research and teaching institutions, including the Mayo Clinic, UCLA Health Center, University of Pennsylvania School of Medicine, and the University of Pittsburgh School of Medicine; governmental agencies, such as the British National Health Service, the National Institutes of Health, U.S. Department of Agriculture, and U.S. Department of Health and Human Services; and even large managed care organizations, such as Kaiser Permanente, *all* acknowledge that a sound vegan diet is perfectly adequate for human health and some of these groups claim that vegan diets may have significant health benefits over diets containing animal products.[1]

It is also the case that there is little, if any, serious disagreement that animal agriculture is resulting in an ecological disaster. Animal agriculture results in the destruction of grasslands and top soil, deforestation, water depletion and pollution, and on all accounts, is a significant contributor to global warming with Worldwatch Institute estimating that 51% of annual worldwide greenhouse gases are attributable to animal agriculture.[2]

In any event, let us focus on veganism as a moral principle.

The word "vegan" was coined by Donald Watson in 1944, coinciding with his founding The Vegan Society in Great Britain. Watson was opposed to animal exploitation and, in the first issue of the Society's newsletter, *The Vegan News*,[3] he wrote, "We can see quite plainly that our present civilisation

---

[1] See Academy of Nutrition and Dietetics (http://www.eatrightpro.org/resource/practice/position-and-practice-papers/position-papers/vegetarian-diets); American Diabetes Association (http://www.diabetes.org/food-and-fitness/food/planning-meals/meal-planning-for-vegetarians); American Heart Association; (http://www.heart.org/HEART-ORG/GettingHealthy/NutritionCenter/Vegetarian-Diets_UCM_306032_Article.jsp); British Dietetic Association (http://www.bda.uk.com/foodfacts/vegetarianfoodfacts.pdf); British National Health Service (http://www.nhs.uk/Livewell/Vegetarianhealth/Pages/Vegandiets.aspx); British Nutrition Foundation (http://www.nutrition.org.uk/publications/briefingpapers/vegetarian-nutrition); Dietary Guidelines of the U.S. Department of Agriculture and U.S. Department of Health and Human Services (http://health.gov/dietaryguidelines/2010); Dieticians Association of Australia (http://daa.asn.au/for-the-public/smart-eating-for-you/nutrition-a-z/vegan-diets); Dieticians of Canada (http://www.dieticians.ca/Your-Health/Nutrition-A-Z/Vegetarian-Diets/Eating-Guidelines-for-Vegans.aspx); Heart and Stroke Foundation (http://www.heartandstroke.com/site/c.ikIQLcMWJtE/b.3484249/k.2F6C/Healthy_living__Vegetarian_diets.htm); Kaiser Permanente (http://www.thepermanentejournal.org/issues/2013/spring/5117-nutrition.html); Mayo Clinic (http://www.mayoclinic.org/healthy-lifestyle/nutrition-and-healthy-eating/in-depth/vegetarian-diet/art-20046446); National Institutes for Health (https://www.nlm.nih.gov/medlineplus/vegetariandiet.html); University of California (Los Angeles) Medical Center (http://www.dining.ucla.edu/housing_site/dining/SNAC_pdf/Vegetarianism.pdf); University of Pennsylvania School of Medicine (http://www.pennmedicine.org/encyclopedia/em_DisplayArticle.aspx?gcid=002465); University of Pittsburgh Medical Center (http://www.upmc.com/health-library/Pages/HealthwiseIndex.aspx?qid=abq2485).

[2] See http://www.worldwatch.org/node/549; http://www.worldwatch.org/node/6294

[3] http://www.abolitionistapproach.com/wp-content/uploads/2015/09/vegan_news_1.pdf

is built on the exploitation of animals, just as past civilisations were built on the exploitation of slaves, and we believe the spiritual destiny of man is such that in time he will view with abhorrence the idea that men once fed on the products of animals' bodies." He maintained that abstaining from meat was not enough, "The unquestionable cruelty associated with the production of dairy produce has made it clear that lacto-vegetarianism is but a half-way house between flesh-eating and a truly humane, civilised diet, and we think, therefore, that during our life on earth we should try to evolve sufficiently to make the 'full journey.'" Watson also rejected eating eggs. "Vegan" comes from the beginning and ending letters of the word "vegetarian," as Watson thought that veganism was the logical place from which vegetarianism stemmed, as well as the point where vegetarianism would ultimately lead. He avoided wearing leather, wool, or silk; and used a fork, rather than a spade, in his gardening to avoid killing worms. Watson was opposed to hunting, fishing, blood sports, and the use of animals in experiments or for testing purposes.

Watson touted (and exemplified) the health benefits of a vegan diet but he clearly saw veganism primarily as a moral principle. He regarded the vegan movement as "the greatest movement that ever was" because it provided a solution to the crisis of greed and violence that affected and afflicted humankind and that threatened ecological disaster. Although he was not religious in a traditional sense, he had deeply held spiritual beliefs, which included the idea that being a nonvegan violated natural law and that, as a general matter, our violence against nonhuman animals was a violation of spiritual laws that resulted in our psychological unhappiness and physical ill-health.

The Abolitionist Approach embraces and develops Watson's position and sees veganism as representing a fundamental moral principle. *The Abolitionist Approach maintains that veganism and creative, nonviolent vegan education are the most important forms of activism and advocacy in which we can engage.* Indeed, it is only through vegan education that we will shift the paradigm away from animals as property and toward animals as persons.

The Abolitionist Approach regards veganism as a *moral imperative.* By this we mean that if animals matter morally, we are morally obligated to stop eating, wearing, and using them. That is, going vegan is not just an option for someone who agrees that animals matter morally; it is a fundamental moral obligation. Abolitionists do not see veganism as a matter of "compassion," "mercy," or anything other than as what is *necessary* to discharge their moral obligations to animals. Similarly, although some people may adopt a vegan diet for health reasons, or out of concern for the environment, an abolitionist vegan sees veganism first and foremost as a matter of moral obligation. It is what they *owe* to animals. An abolitionist vegan may have health or environmental concerns as well, but the primary motivating force for the abolitionist vegan is morality.

The Abolitionist Approach is clear: *if one is not a vegan, one is participating actively in animal exploitation.* Since abolitionists reject *all* animal exploitation, even supposedly "humane" exploitation, abolitionists have no choice but to be principled and consistent vegans.

Abolitionists see veganism as a rejection of the status of nonhuman animals as commodities. Humans exploit animals because they are viewed as things. They are property without moral value. Abolitionists reject the property status of nonhuman animals and refuse to participate in their institutionalized commodification. Abolitionists recognize that every time humans eat, wear, or use an animal product, they are reaffirming the insidious system that treats nonhuman animals exclusively as resources for humans.

Abolitionists see veganism as representing a fundamental principle of justice: it is simply unfair to treat nonhumans as replaceable resources, and to deny them the one right that we accord all humans irrespective of particular characteristics.

Abolitionists see veganism as an act of nonviolent defiance, as a refusal to participate in the oppression of the innocent and the vulnerable, and as a rejection of the insidious idea that harming other sentient beings should be considered as a "normal" part of life.

Abolitionists see veganism as applying the principle of abolition to one's life. Animal advocates who claim to favor animal rights and to want to abolish animal exploitation but who continue to eat or use animal products are no different from those who claimed to be in favor of human rights and the abolition of slavery but who continued to own slaves.

Abolitionists see veganism as a necessary element of a nonviolent life. That is, if someone embraces nonviolence, they have an obligation to be vegan. They must also embrace nonviolence in other ways: veganism is not sufficient but it certainly is necessary.

From the foregoing, it should be clear that, as far as abolitionists are concerned, veganism applies not just to diet but to wearing or using animals. In other words, a vegan is one who does not eat, wear, or use animals in their life to the extent practicable. It is impossible to avoid all animal products. Given that we kill billions of animals every year, animal by-products are available cheaply and are included in many things, such as road surfaces, plastics, and in glues used to make shoes. But when we do have a choice—and that is just about always, unless we are on a desert island or shipwrecked—we are morally obligated not to eat, wear, or use animals. We also believe that veganism means not participating in or patronizing activities that involve animal exploitation, such as circuses, zoos, rodeos, or horse racing.

We do not believe, however, that veganism is synonymous with "everything morally good." Although we talk about the rejection of human discrimination and it is an element of the Abolitionist Approach (see our discussion of *Principle Five*), we think it unhelpful to say, for example, that a person who is sexist is not a vegan. A person who is sexist is not an abolitionist as we use that term. But a sexist can be a sexist vegan. There is a tendency on the part of some vegans to use the term so broadly that it becomes shorthand for all the elements of that person's view of ideal morality. That simply causes confusion.

Vegetarianism as a "Gateway"?

Although, as a moral matter, Watson rejected the consumption of all animal products, he thought that, as a psychological and sociological matter, it was necessary for people to pass through a period of vegetarianism first before they became vegan. He saw vegetarianism as a sort of "gateway" because he saw veganism as representing the conclusion of an evolutionary process that started with vegetarianism. Watson did not object to vegans promoting vegetarianism precisely because he viewed it as an essential part of this evolutionary process.

Abolitionists reject this notion and maintain that we should be clear that vegetarianism involves animal exploitation and must be rejected. There is no morally coherent distinction between flesh and other animal products. Promoting vegetarianism as part of an "evolution" supposedly culminating in veganism is equivalent to saying that we ought to promote consuming some animal products as a way of eliminating the consumption of all animal products. In this sense, the "gateway" argument concerning vegetarianism is exactly the same as the argument for welfare reform: that we should promote "humane" exploitation as a way of supposedly achieving no exploitation. Abolitionists reject the "gateway" argument in both contexts.

If humans and nonhumans are all equal in holding a right not to be used as property, then just as *any* sort of human slavery is a violation of that right, so is *any* sort of animal exploitation a violation of it. Abolitionists do not promote vegetarianism because there is no morally coherent distinction between flesh and other animal products. There is no coherent distinction between meat and dairy or eggs. Animals exploited in the dairy and egg industries live longer, are treated worse, and end up in the same slaughterhouse as their counterparts killed for meat. To not eat beef but still drink milk makes as little sense as eating flesh from large cows but not from small cows. Moreover, there is also no morally relevant distinction between a cow and a fish for purposes of treating either as a human resource. We may more easily recognize the pain or suffering of a cow because, like us, she is a mammal. But that is not a reason to ignore the suffering and death of the many billions of sentient fish and other sea animals whom we kill annually.

Abolitionists do not promote campaigns like Meatless Monday, which, among other things, reinforce the idea that there is something morally worse in eating flesh than in eating dairy or eggs. *All* animal products involve suffering; they *all* involve death; they *all* involve injustice. Veganism is a moral imperative; it is what we *ought* to do and we ought not to do anything less.

Beyond Being Vegan: Creative, Nonviolent Vegan Education

The more people embrace abolitionist veganism, the stronger will be the cultural notion that animals have a moral right not to be treated as commodities. If we are ever going to end animal exploitation, it is imperative that there be a social and political movement that actively seeks abolition and regards veganism as its moral baseline. As long as the majority of people think that eating animals and animal products is a morally acceptable behavior, nothing will change. There may be a larger selection of "happy meat" and other fare for affluent "conscientious omnivores" or "compassionate consumers," but this will not abolish animal exploitation or do anything other than make society more comfortable with exploitation and thereby entrench it more deeply.

The most important form of incremental change on a social level is creative, nonviolent education about veganism and the need to abolish, not regulate, the institutionalized exploitation of animals. The Abolitionist Approach strongly endorses Nelson Mandela's position, "Education is the most powerful weapon which you can use to change the world."

Veganism and creative, positive, nonviolent vegan education provide practical and incremental strategies both in terms of reducing animal suffering now and in terms of building a movement that will be able to obtain more meaningful legislation in the form of rights-based prohibitions of animal use rather than "humane" welfare regulation or SICs that represent counterproductive coalitions. If, in the late 1980s—when the animal advocacy community in the United States decided very deliberately to pursue a welfarist agenda rather than an abolitionist one—a substantial portion of movement resources had been invested in vegan education and advocacy, there would likely be many hundreds of thousands more vegans today. That is a very conservative estimate given the many millions of dollars that have been expended by animal advocacy groups to promote welfarist legislation and initiatives. By promoting veganism as a moral baseline and decreasing demand for animal products, the increased number of vegans would have reduced suffering far more than have all of the supposed welfarist successes put together. Although estimates vary, a vegan saves about 200 animals per year.

Increasing the number of vegans would also help build a political and economic base required for the social change that is a necessary predicate for legal change. Given that there is limited time, and there are limited financial resources available, expansion of animal welfare is not a rational and efficient choice if we seek abolition in the long term. Indeed, traditional animal welfare is not an effective way of reducing animal suffering in the short term.

Moreover, it is important for animal advocates to be engaged in efforts to educate society at all levels and through all media about animal exploitation and the moral basis for its abolition. At the present time, the prevailing moral norm, reflected in the law, is that it is morally acceptable to use nonhumans for human purposes as long as animals are treated "humanely." As a result of this, the social debate focuses on what constitutes "humane" treatment, and many advocates spend their time trying to convince members of the public that larger cages are better than smaller cages or that gassing chickens is better than slitting their throats. But that is all wrong: the debate should be shifted in the direction of animal use and the indisputable fact that humans have no coherent moral justification for continuing to use nonhumans, however "humanely" they are treated. This requires that advocates educate themselves about the ethical arguments against animal use and that they engage in creative ways to make those arguments accessible to the general public. Given that most people accept that nonhumans are members of the moral community in some sense—that is, they already at least reject the notion that animals are merely things—it is challenging, but not impossible, to get people to see that membership in the moral community means that we stop using animals altogether.

What is important is that in educating people about veganism, we should emphasize that it is animal *use* and not animal *treatment* that is the primary problem. That is, arguments about veganism should not be based on whether animals are abused in particular ways or at particular facilities. The issue is not whether the animals are confined in an intensive facility or whether they are sent to a slaughterhouse where workers kick them in addition to the other horrible things that they do to them as part of the standard slaughter process. The point is that we cannot justify treating animals as commodities and killing them for our purposes irrespective of how the animals are treated.

The most important form of vegan education is the sort that *anyone* can do and can do *today*—talking with neighbors, colleagues, family, friends, etc.

In order to see the power of this form of advocacy, let us hypothesize that there are presently 2 million vegans in the United States (a low estimate). If every one of those 2 million vegans persuaded one other person to go vegan in the next year, there would be 4 million vegans. And if we repeat this each year (with each vegan persuading another to go vegan) the entire country would be vegan in less than a decade. The lowest estimate of vegans in the United Kingdom is 150,000. It would take a decade to achieve a vegan Britain if every vegan persuaded one person per year to go vegan.

Creative, nonviolent vegan advocacy can take many forms, limited only by the imagination. For example, tabling at local markets and fairs, or just on the street—where you can talk with people, provide them with information about animal rights and veganism, and, perhaps, even share a sample of vegan food with them—is a particularly effective way to educate. There are a number of abolitionist vegans who do this sort of thing on a regular basis and they have reported tremendous success in persuading people that veganism is a moral imperative and that they ought to go vegan. Giving presentations about abolitionist veganism at local schools, colleges, and universities, as well as to other groups in your community, is another great way of doing vegan education. These are just a few examples of creative abolitionist advocacy. There are many others.

We often find that it is useful to focus the discussion on eating animals because until people see the immorality of eating meat, dairy, eggs, and other animal products, they are unlikely to see the problems with using animals in other contexts. Once a person stops eating animals and animal products, all of their choices will change. Someone who understands the argument we make and stops eating animals will stop purchasing animal clothing and supporting any activity that involves animals.

We are often asked about our views on demonstrations. Demonstrations are great if they focus on veganism and veganism alone. "Veg" or "Veggie Pride" demonstrations just confuse things because they promote vegetarianism as well as veganism. That sends the message that vegetarianism is the baseline and veganism goes beyond the baseline—and that is the wrong message to send.

But we sincerely believe that talking to your friends, relatives, neighbors, and to those in your community is the very best thing to do. Keep in mind that if you and every vegan just persuaded one other person to go vegan in the next year, we would shift the paradigm in the direction of nonhuman personhood fairly quickly.

Before you go out and advocate, it is imperative, however, that you educate yourself. In order to be an effective teacher, you must first be a diligent student. Many animal advocates want to be "activists" but have no idea about the substantive arguments in favor of abolitionist veganism. They can end up doing more harm than good. You don't have to have a PhD in philosophy in order to educate, but you must be reasonably familiar with the arguments in favor of abolition and you must be able to talk with people in situations that may sometimes be stressful. We wrote this book and our earlier book, *Eat Like You Care: An Examination of the Morality of Eating Animals,* in part to help educate you, the reader, so that you can educate others. Take advantage of the free resources that we make available on our websites:

www.AbolitionistApproach.com

www.HowDoIGoVegan.com

In addition to the substantive material contained in these books and on our sites, we offer the following five general guiding ideas to help shape any advocacy you do:

Advocacy Guide #1: People are good at heart.

Our default position when we talk with people ought to be that they are good at heart, and interested in, and educable about, moral issues. There is a tendency among at least some advocates to have a very misanthropic view of other humans and to see them as being inherently immoral or uninterested in issues of morality. We disagree with that view.

Advocacy Guide #2: People are not stupid.

Many animal advocates believe that the general public is not able to understand the arguments in favor of veganism and that, because of this, we must not promote veganism directly. They claim that instead of talking about veganism, we should talk about vegetarianism, Meatless Monday, "happy" meat and other animal products, and just about anything except veganism. For example, Ronnie Lee, a prominent British animal advocate and founder of the Animal Liberation Front, maintains that "we need to take into account the limitations of ordinary people" because they do not possess the requisite "intellectual and moral abilities" needed to understand veganism as a moral imperative. Tony Wardle, co-founder of Viva!, an animal organization that is based in Britain but has been actively involved in promoting "happy" exploitation in the United States, claims that "single mums" can't grasp the idea of veganism as a moral principle.[4] We disagree strongly with this very elitist way of thinking about other people. There is no mystery here; there is nothing complicated. People can understand if we teach effectively. The problem is not "ordinary people." The problem is so-called animal advocates who are unwilling to promote veganism as a moral baseline.

Advocacy Guide #3: Do not get defensive; respond, don't react.

Yes, some people will try to provoke us or will ask questions or make comments that we will find insulting or that we will take as not being serious. If someone is really not interested in what we are saying, they will, as a general matter, walk away. Treat every comment and question—even the ones you find abrasive, rude, or sarcastic—as an *invitation* being offered to you by someone who is more provoked (in a positive way) by you and more engaged than you might think.

Advocacy Guide #4: Do not get frustrated. Education is hard work.

You will get the same question many times; you will be asked questions that indicate you must start at the beginning with someone. But if you want to be an effective educator, you have to answer every question as if it were the first time you heard it. If you want others to be enthusiastic about your message, *you* have to be enthusiastic about it first.

---

[4]Lee and Wardle are discussed, and their comments cited, here: http://www.abolitionistapproach.com/vegan-elitism-ronnie-lee-on-ordinary-people

Advocacy Guide #5: Learn the basics. You have to be a student first before you become a teacher.

Many animal advocates become excited about abolitionist veganism and the next thing that happens is that they set up a website or start a blog that is motivated by the right feelings but not informed by clear ideas. Before you teach others, learn the basics. This is the most important idea to keep in mind: The Abolitionist Approach is a *grassroots movement*. Advocating veganism as a fundamental principle of justice is not something that requires large, wealthy charities and corporate "leaders." It is something that we can do and *must* do as a grassroots movement. Each one of us must be a leader by educating in a clear and unequivocal way about veganism as a moral imperative and the abolition of exploitation as a fundamental matter of the right of all sentient beings to not be used as things. But we must each spend the time needed so that we can be effective educators.

The Modern "Animal Movement": The Rejection of Veganism

All of the large animal organizations reject veganism as a moral baseline. *All of them.* That statement may be shocking but, unfortunately, it is true.

To the extent that these organizations promote veganism (and many do not promote veganism at all), they do so as a way—*one way*—of reducing suffering. That is, they present veganism as a way to reduce suffering along with many other ways, such as consuming cage-free eggs, crate-free pork, animal products with one of the many "happy" labels, meat from a slaughterhouse designed or approved by Temple Grandin (to whom People for the Ethical Treatment of Animals (PETA) gave an award), or any animal product other than foie gras. That is, these organizations do not promote veganism as a moral baseline. They do not send out the message that if you are not vegan, you are engaged in animal exploitation, which is immoral. According to the new welfarists, if X decides to supposedly reduce suffering on Monday by eating no meat but eating other animal products, that's a good step. To maintain that, as a moral matter, X should be a vegan on *all* days is, according to the new welfarists, "absolutist," "fundamentalist," or "fanatical." Indeed, the new welfarists explicitly argue that people should not be vegan if it makes others feel uncomfortable.

The origin of this rejection of veganism as a moral imperative is found in the position of Peter Singer. We encountered Singer earlier when we discussed his rejection of the idea that we should accord animals a moral right not to be used as things or as resources for humans. We saw that Singer is a utilitarian who rejects rights generally for both nonhumans and humans, but that he accords rights-like protection to normal humans because they are supposedly cognitively more sophisticated than nonhumans, who, Singer believes, have no interest in continued existence, or, if they do, have an interest that is qualitatively different from the interest that normal humans have. Singer's position on animal advocacy is that advocates should support *any* measure that supposedly lessens suffering. In this approach, veganism *cannot* be a moral baseline. There is no moral baseline as far as advocacy is concerned. There are only measures that supposedly reduce suffering and Singer supports all of them. Veganism reduces suffering but so does, according to Singer, the "enriched" battery cage and other welfarist measures.

Singer claims that being a "conscientious omnivore" is a "defensible ethical position" and that those concerned about animal ethics can indulge in "the luxury of free range eggs, or possibly even meat from animals who live good lives under conditions natural for their species, and are then humanely killed on the farm." Singer describes himself as a "flexible vegan" who may not eat vegan when traveling or visiting others. He argues that when one orders a vegan meal in a restaurant, but it comes with animal products in it, sending it back results in wasting food, and states that "if you're in company with people who are not vegan or not even vegetarian, I think that's probably the wrong thing to do. It'd be better off just to eat it because people are going to think, 'Oh my god, these vegans . . .'" He calls being a consistent vegan "fanatical."[5]

Singer's ideas are pervasive among the large groups. For example, PETA's Ingrid Newkirk has expressed support for "flexitarianism" or part-time vegetarianism, calling those who advocate for veganism as a baseline moral principle "[a]bsolute purists." With respect to the principle of veganism as a moral imperative, she says, "Screw the principle."[6] PETA discourages people from "grilling waiters at restaurants" about small amounts of animal products in food because that may make "sticking to a vegetarian diet seem difficult and dogmatic to your friends and to restaurant staff, thus discouraging them from giving a vegetarian diet a try." PETA also urges people not to insist that their food be cooked separately from animal foods because "doing so doesn't help any additional animals, and it only makes restaurants less inclined to offer vegetarian choices."[7]

This rejection of veganism as a moral baseline by calling it "purism" or harmful to animals is explicitly embraced by Farm Sanctuary, Mercy for Animals, Compassion Over Killing, Vegan Outreach, Sea Shepherd, and by just about every large so-called animal advocacy group out there.[8] Even

---

[5] For the links to Singer's quotes, see http://www.abolitionistapproach.com/peter-singer-oh-my-god-these-vegans

[6] http://www.abolitionistapproach.com/ingrid-newkirk-on-principled-veganism-screw-the-principle

[7] http://www.peta.org/living/food/making-transition-vegetarian/ideas-vegetarian-living/tiny-amount-animal-products-food

[8] See these essays: http://www.abolitionistapproach.com/animal-welfare-regulation-happy-exploitation-and-speciesism/; http://www.abolitionistapproach.com/sea-shepherd-

The Vegan Society has rejected veganism as a moral baseline.[9] Some groups have taken an even more extreme position, such as the Humane Society of the United States, which not only does not promote veganism as a moral baseline, but also employs a pig farmer, Joe Maxwell, as Political Director of its Legislative Fund (and a former Vice President), distributes discount coupons for "happy" meat items, and sponsors events where the corpses of "happy" animals are served.[10] Direct Action Everywhere, a relative newcomer to the scene, claims that advocating veganism is "harmful."[11]

These groups point out that we cannot live without harming any animals in that animals are killed and injured in the growing and harvesting of crops, and so even if we all ate plants, some animals would still be harmed. They also claim that, because we cannot avoid all animal by-products or ingredients, which are in things like road surfaces and plastics, "perfection" is not possible and so we should not promote veganism. But that position is just nonsense. *All* human activity involves indirect harm. That is, everything we do has consequences and some of those consequences are adverse. For example, every product we consume involves a manufacturing process, which invariably results in some amount of unintentional harm, including death, to those who participate in that manufacturing process. So should we say that, because we cannot avoid harm to other humans even if we consume as little as possible, we ought to not advocate against human slavery? Of course not. But that is *exactly* what these so-called animal advocates are saying we should do in the animal context. They maintain that, because we cannot avoid harming animals unintentionally, we ought not to advocate against the deliberate commodification of animals incidental to their status as human property. It is transparently clear that this "perfection" argument is really about promoting the welfarist position that since we cannot avoid all harm, the best we can do is to supposedly lessen harm, so all ways of what they claim to lessen harm, including consuming "happy" animal products,

weighs-in-on-cecil-the-lion-insisting-on-veganism-is-purism-and-elitist

[9] http://www.abolitionistapproach.com/banned-by-the-vegan-society-for-promoting-veganism

[10] http://www.abolitionistapproach.com/animal-welfare-regulation-happy-exploitation-and-speciesism (Maxwell and the other HSUS matters are discussed toward the end of the cited essay.)

[11] http://www.abolitionistapproach.com/direct-action-everywhere-dxe-vegan-advocacy-is-harmful-to-the-animal-rights-movement

are legitimate moral responses. This position bolsters the ability of the large animal charities to fundraise off welfare reform campaigns.

In short, the modern "animal movement" has explicitly rejected veganism as a moral baseline.

As we saw in our discussion of *Principle Two,* and as we will see further in our discussion of *Principle Four,* a fundamental assumption[12] of the welfarist position is that killing animals does not per se inflict a harm on them. According to this view, animals do not care *that* we use and kill them; they only care about *how* we treat them and kill them. As long as they don't suffer "too much," (whatever that means) animals are indifferent to our using them because they have no interest in continued existence. It is this thinking that has led to the "happy" meat/animal products movement,[13] which has been the most serious setback in the struggle for justice for nonhumans in decades. The focus of the "happy exploitation" movement is exclusively on suffering, and so those who support that approach will promote any measure that they believe will reduce suffering. This can include, but is not limited to, veganism. But the welfarist position necessarily rejects veganism as a moral baseline.

Abolitionists reject this position and maintain that we can no more justify using nonhumans as human resources than we can justify human slavery. Animal use and slavery have at least one important point in common: both institutions treat sentient beings exclusively as resources of others. Slavery cannot be justified with respect to humans and it cannot be justified with respect to nonhumans—*however* "humanely" we treat either the human slaves or the animal property. Veganism is not just a way of reducing suffering; it is a commitment to justice and an explicit refusal to participate in animal slavery.

The Abolitionist Approach sees veganism as the application of the principle of abolition to the life of the individual. It is our expression that we embrace the moral personhood of all sentient beings and we reject the status of nonhumans as chattel property. Veganism is not just a way of reducing suffering; it is what justice for nonhumans *requires.* It is not the last step in a

---

[12] See http://www.abolitionistapproach.com/peter-singer-and-the-welfarist-position-on-the-lesser-value-of-nonhuman-life

[13] See http://www.abolitionistapproach.com/happy-meat-making-humans-feel-better-about-eating-animals

journey to reject the moral schizophrenia—or the completely delusional way of thinking, which characterizes the human/nonhuman relationship—it is the *first* step. If animals have any moral significance, then we cannot eat, wear, or use them. A vegan is not a vegan only on Mondays, or only when it is convenient. *A vegan is a vegan all the time.* We would no more fail to be vegan just because our being vegan made someone else uncomfortable than we would remain silent if someone told a racist joke or harassed a woman because to object would make the perpetrator uncomfortable. It is no more "absolutist" or "fanatical" to be a consistent vegan than it is to be consistent in one's rejection of rape or pedophilia. Indeed, to characterize consistent veganism as "absolutist" is itself speciesist precisely because we would not so characterize our complete rejection of fundamental forms of human exploitation.

The new welfarists are unwilling to take the position that veganism is a moral imperative because they are unwilling to say that consuming animal products is categorically wrong. Instead, they promote the idea that it's all about being on a "journey" and that we cannot make value judgments about other people's "journeys." When this is challenged, they claim that since most vegans were not vegan from birth, vegans have no right to criticize those who are not yet vegan. But this misses the point. Imagine someone saying, "It took me a while to stop being a racist so I think that the civil rights movement should promote the idea that it's fine for everyone to learn to embrace equality at their own pace. If someone thinks that it's okay to discriminate against people of color, we cannot make judgments. To say that equality is an unequivocal moral baseline is to take a 'my way or the highway' approach. We need baby steps. Let's start with Racist-Joke-Free Monday." If someone said that, we would think that such a person was *seriously* confused and did not understand the nature of morality.

We should, of course, always seek to teach others in a nonviolent manner. But we have an *obligation* to the animals to be crystal clear that the moral status of nonhumans means that *any* exploitation, irrespective of how "humane" it is, is morally unjustifiable. Some so-called animal advocates claim that clarity is inconsistent with nonviolence. We disagree. We would never say that racism (or sexism, or homophobia, or any other sort of human discrimination) is acceptable if it is "humane" or if we eliminate the "worst abuses." We would never say that we should "meet racists (or sexists, or heterosexists) where they are" and respect that they are on a "journey." Being crystal clear in the animal context is what nonviolence requires.

A variant of the "journey" argument is the position that "we can't tell people what to do." This position is articulated by many new welfarists. But how can we have a social justice movement for animals if we *don't* maintain that we must be clear with people as to what is morally obligatory with respect to animals? There is *nothing* violent or aggressive about being clear. Indeed, to not be clear is to not only disrespect the animals but also to disrespect the person with whom we are talking. We owe them the truth about the immorality of animal exploitation. If they hear our message and are concerned but do not go vegan or do not do so immediately, that should be *their* choice and not anything that *we* advise as morally acceptable or desirable. Abolitionists maintain that animal advocates should never advise as morally acceptable the consumption of any animal products.

Abolitionists maintain that we have a moral obligation to be crystal clear about the immorality of animal exploitation. Abolitionists are moral realists. Moral realism is the position that moral facts and moral values exist as objective truths that are independent of our perception of them, or of our beliefs or attitudes about these facts and values. When we say, "There is a cup on the table," in a situation in which there is, in fact, a cup on the table, we mean that statement to be true. It's not a matter of beliefs or attitudes; it's a matter of fact. A moral realist would say, for example, that statements like, "Genocide is bad," or "It is wrong to torture a child," are true in the way that the statement about the cup is true.

Abolitionists maintain that the statement, "It is wrong to treat nonhumans as things and exclusively as resources for humans," is not a matter of belief or attitude; it is a matter of truth. Any position, including but not limited to, the animal welfare position or any position that promotes animal exploitation—even if it is a supposed means to the end of abolishing animal exploitation—conflicts with this fundamental moral reality.

Moral realism is not as mysterious as it may seem. Most people would say, for example, that the morality of the Holocaust is not a matter of belief or attitude and that there is a clear moral truth about this event—that it was wrong. Similarly, is the morality of torturing or sexually molesting a child a matter of attitude or belief? Most of us would say it is just wrong to torture or molest a child even if a particular person thought it was alright to do so, just as we would say that, "The cup is on the table" is true if there was, in fact, a cup on the table and even if Joe said that there was no cup on the table. Although we would say that imposing less suffering on a child being tortured is "better" than imposing more suffering, we would not promote torturing the child as itself morally desirable. That is, we would not campaign for "humane" child molestation. Because abolitionists reject speciesism, they regard animal exploitation in the same way. It is always better to inflict less suffering on animals than more suffering, but abolitionists should not affirmatively promote "humane" animal exploitation any more than they should support "humane" child molestation, even though it is better to inflict less harm on a child than more harm. To promote "humane" animal exploitation would contravene the basic moral principle that the abolitionist embraces—that it is morally wrong to use nonhuman animals as resources for humans.

As mentioned earlier, some welfarists maintain that we cannot tell people what to do. It is certainly the case that we cannot force others not to act in ways that they are allowed to act. If someone wants to eat animals, we cannot make them not do so. But if we really embrace the idea that animals have rights and that veganism is a moral imperative, we not only can, but we are under an obligation to, make clear to others that the exploitation of animals, however "humane," is morally unjustifiable. And it's not a matter of judging others; it's a matter of judging actions. The former is never a good idea; the latter is essential if we are going to have a social justice movement for animals.

The Newest New Welfarist Strategy: Promoting "Reducetarianism" (and "Happy Exploitation") is More "Effective" than Promoting Veganism

In our discussion of *Principle Two,* we saw that welfarists have attempted unsuccessfully to claim that "science" shows that welfare reform campaigns cause people to consume less meat. But the main focus of the welfarists in the use of science to "prove" that they are right and abolitionists are wrong concerns veganism. The welfarists claim that "science" shows that promoting nonveganism will be more "effective" at getting people to go vegan and that, in any event, promoting the reduction of meat-eating will reduce animal suffering more than promoting veganism. Interestingly, the welfarists appear to be conceding that the abolitionists are right on the moral issues. Indeed, they have, for the most part, given up even trying to argue the moral point that we are morally obligated to go vegan just as we are morally obligated not to own slaves or discriminate against people of color or women. They claim, however, that although abolitionists may be right morally, it is the welfarist position that is "effective." "Effective" has become the new buzz word of the welfarist movement. In the words of welfarist Melanie Joy, "It is better to be effective than to be right."[14]

There is now a growing industry of supposedly "independent research organizations" which produces what purports to be research that allegedly shows that promoting veganism is not as effective in persuading people to become vegans as is promoting "reducetarianism," (i.e., the idea that people should consume less meat) or some form of "happy" exploitation. These groups include Faunalytics (formerly known as the Humane Research Council), the Humane League Labs, and Animal Charity Evaluators. These groups have yet to produce a *single* peer-reviewed study—or *any* study that is methodologically sound—which shows that promoting nonveganism is more effective than promoting veganism. Dr. Casey Taft, Professor of Psychiatry at Boston University School of Medicine; an expert on how to promote behavior change as well as on research method design; an author of more than 100 journal articles, book chapters, and scientific reports (most of which were peer reviewed); and the associate editor of the journal, *Psychological Trauma: Theory, Research, Practice, and Policy,* calls the "research" produced by these groups "pseudoscience." Dr. Taft has written excellent essays that completely debunk the claims of these organizations and make clear that there is *no* evidence to support the claims of these so-called "independent research organizations."[15] For example, Dr. Taft points out that in one study done by Faunalytics, "their data actually showed the opposite of their conclusions and indicated that we should truly be promoting veganism rather than 'reducetarianism.'"

---

[14]Joy is quoted in this essay: http://dailypitchfork.org/?p=625
[15]See, e.g., http://veganpublishers.com/animal-advocacy-and-the-scientific-method-the-humane-research-council-study/; http://veganpublishers.com/pseudoscience/; and http://veganpublishers.com/effectiveness

In order to see what Taft means when he refers to this supposed "empirical" work as "pseudoscience," consider a "study" that was done by the Humane League Labs, which is part of a welfarist group called the Humane League. The authors wanted to see whether people would respond better to a message about animal cruelty (the usual approach taken by the welfarist groups that promote supposedly more "humane" exploitation), the environment, or the "purity" position, which is the denigrating term used by the "researchers" to describe the abolitionist or animal rights position.[16] Right from the outset, the welfarist authors do not even try to hide their obvious bias.

So what did the authors do to see which approach would get the best response? They made three short pamphlets that focused on animal cruelty, "purity," and the environment. *That's right, the welfarists made the pamphlets.* The welfarists decided how abolitionists presented their position. The welfarists then distributed these pamphlets. We could not find anything that discussed how the pamphlets were distributed so we asked the Humane League and were told in an email that "[p]articipants were recruited online via Amazon Mechanical Turk, and the flyers and questions were presented online." So they did a study to measure the effectiveness of advocacy by doing it entirely online? That's interesting. The welfarists then asked the participants about whether they intended to reduce their consumption of animal products in the coming month. The welfarists made various assumptions about how the stated intention would translate into actual behavioral change and concocted a scale that provided a number of "days of animal suffering," and concluded that the "purist" or abolitionist position led to fewer "days of animal suffering spared" than the other two approaches.

Interestingly, the control group used in the "study" received no flyer at all and they stated an intention to reduce their consumption more than those who received any of the three pamphlets. The only conclusions one can draw from this are that the material that the welfarists distributed were completely ineffective or their research design was seriously flawed. This did not stop the authors from concluding that asking others to reduce consumption was more effective than asking people to recognize veganism as a moral imperative.

It does not require expertise in research methods to conclude that this

---

[16] See https://humaneleaguelabs.wordpress.com/2015/09/20/report-is-animal-cruelty-or-purity-abolitionist-messaging-more-effective

is, as Dr. Taft says, "pseudoscience." A welfarist group decided how to characterize and present the abolitionist position and they distributed the pamphlets they designed to an online group with a control group that had a more positive response than any of those who received any of the pamphlets. The authors then "discovered" that people responded better to the welfarist position that the Humane League and other welfarist groups promote. The Humane League did not submit this study for peer review, which is standard practice in the scientific community. That is because *no* reputable journal would have published this nonsense. Taft notes that "when determining how best to encourage people to stop exploiting animals, they ask those doing the exploiting how we should craft our message to them." He comments:

> Let that sink in for a moment and ask yourself how that would look with any other social justice movement. Do you think the Black Lives Matter folks conduct surveys with white racists in an effort to determine how we can end racial injustice? Do feminists conduct focus groups with sexist men about how we can best end patriarchy and violence against women? Of course not! It is absurd to ask those doing the oppressing how we should talk to them to encourage them to stop the oppression.[17]

The idea that promoting nonveganism is more "effective" than promoting veganism if you want people to go vegan is counterintuitive in the same way that the idea that promoting "gentle" sexism and misogyny is more "effective" in achieving gender equality than is being clear that sexism and misogyny are morally wrong, or the idea that promoting "gentle" racism is more "effective" in achieving racial equality than is promoting the idea that racism is morally wrong. And there is *no* empirical evidence whatsoever that supports this counterintuitive position.

In addition to the fact that no empirical evidence supports the welfarist position that promoting nonveganism will lead to people going vegan more effectively than educating them about veganism directly, it must be understood that the large welfarist groups have *never* promoted veganism as a moral baseline and have for many years been promoting the ideas that are the very sources of the false and predominant public view that veganism

---

[17] http://veganpublishers.com/advocacy

is "extreme" and that people can't cope with the message. Moreover, many, if not the great majority, of the members of these welfare groups are not even vegan themselves (and by vegan we mean *consistently* so; "flexible veganism" that depends on convenience of all sorts is *not* veganism). So, it is not surprising that the large groups are promoting the idea that veganism is "extreme," and that they then claim that people think that veganism is "extreme," which is what these groups use as "empirical proof" that people won't respond to a vegan message. In other words, the large welfarist groups claim that the public regards veganism as "extreme," whereas these same groups do not acknowledge that *they* are the ones largely responsible for persuading the public to adopt such a false view.

In response to welfarist Melanie Joy's statement, "It is better to be effective than to be right," we reply that the position that Joy and other welfarists support is neither right nor effective.

We saw in our discussion of *Principle Two* that it makes no sense morally or practically to promote a strategy or means that is fundamentally inconsistent with the ends we profess to seek. "Reducetarianism" is such a strategy or means. Although many advocates of this position do not embrace veganism and promote "reducetarianism" for environmental or health reasons, or, supposedly, to reduce animal suffering, some animal advocates promote it as a strategy that they claim with lead to veganism.

Putting aside that the "reducetarian" position almost always focuses on meat and completely ignores dairy, eggs, and other animal products, as well as ignores the use of animals for clothing and other purposes, this position is morally objectionable because, like promoting "happy" exploitation as a supposed means to no exploitation, it promotes what it claims to be a lesser degree of exploitation as a morally acceptable way of discharging our moral obligations to animals. Those who promote "reducetarianism" reject promoting the idea that people are obligated to go vegan and, instead, claim that people can satisfy their moral obligations by reducing their intake of meat. That is like saying that we reject promoting that people are morally obligated to stop engaging in sexual violence against women and that they can satisfy their moral obligations to women by reducing their violence. Although less violence against women is better than more, *no one* would think it morally acceptable to advocate a "gentle" rape campaign.

Moreover, as a practical matter, the "reducetarian" position—that we should promote reducing exploitation to people who care about animals rather than promote abolishing exploitation—is absurd. Think about it: if someone cares about animals and hears the vegan message but does not want to go vegan, that person will decide on their own to eat less meat or consume fewer animal products. That is, if they think, "Yes, it's right that we shouldn't be exploiting animals but I'm not going to go vegan at least for now," that person will most likely reduce their consumption of animal products. But animal advocates who take animal rights seriously should never say that reducing animal consumption is an alternative to veganism as far as moral obligations are concerned. That will ensure that people will *never* go vegan.

When we do vegan advocacy, we often encounter people who say that they are concerned about animals and would like to go vegan but say they are not, for various reasons, ready to do so immediately. We always reassure these people that it is easy to go vegan and we provide them with resources (such as www.HowIGoVegan.com) so that they can see that going vegan is not at all difficult. If, however, they insist they are not going to go vegan immediately and ask for an "incremental" approach, we advise that they try going vegan for breakfast for a week or two, and then add vegan lunches for a week or two, and then dinners. (We also advise that in any future purchase of clothes or personal care products, they do not purchase animal products.) *But we are always clear that veganism is the moral imperative and any animal products that they consume over those six (or however many) weeks until they stop consuming animals altogether represents a violation of the fundamental rights of animals.* We do not, and never would, say that any consumption is itself a morally acceptable thing. On the contrary, it is not.

We cannot emphasize enough that animal advocates should always be clear that veganism is a moral imperative. It is not an optional matter; it is a matter of our moral obligation to animals. If someone cares morally about animals but wants to do less, let that be *their* choice and not what *we* promote.

Conclusion

A fundamental tenet of the Abolitionist Approach to Animal Rights is that if animals matter morally and are not just things, we cannot justify eating, wearing, or using them. Veganism is not an option; it is a moral imperative, and any movement that seeks justice for nonhumans must promote veganism as a baseline.

As we saw above, some who are vegans for moral reasons see veganism only as a way of reducing animal suffering and may, therefore, eat or use an animal product if they think that more suffering will be caused otherwise. These vegans are often "flexible" vegans, which, in our view, means that they are not vegans. An abolitionist vegan sees veganism as a general approach to life—a philosophy of living—and not merely as a matter of lifestyle.

We note that, in our experience, abolitionist veganism is the *only* approach that results in consistent behavior. Those who adopt a vegan diet for health reasons alone often "cheat" just as those who are on any diet for health reasons often do. Those who adopt a vegan diet for environmental reasons may not only lapse but may decide that an animal product has fewer adverse environmental consequences than non-animal products. And in both cases, veganism is seen merely as a diet and not as a fundamental principle of justice that applies not just to animals exploited for food but also to animals used for clothing, product ingredients, and other uses. This does not mean that an abolitionist vegan is not concerned about health and the environment. On the contrary, we feel that our commitment to nonviolence *requires* that we act mindfully with respect to our own health and toward the environment, on which all sentient beings depend.

But ultimately, abolitionist veganism is rooted in a position of animal ethics that is fundamentally committed to bringing justice to nonhuman animals.

Further Reading

Books

Gary L. Francione and Anna Charlton, *Eat Like You Care: An Examination of the Morality of Eating Animals* (Exempla Press 2013).
Gary L. Francione & Robert Garner, *The Animal Rights Debate: Abolition or Regulation?* (Columbia University Press 2010), 62-74.

Essays

Gary L. Francione, "Animal Welfare, Happy Meat, and Veganism as a Moral Baseline," in *The Philosophy of Food,* ed. David Kaplan (University of California Press, 2012).

Blog Posts

"Veganism Without Animal Rights" (with Anna Charlton), at
www.theeuropean-magazine.com/gary-l-francione/10366-the-morality-of-eating-meat-eggs-and-dairy
"Some Thoughts on the Meaning of 'Vegan,'" at
www.abolitionistapproach.com/some-thoughts-on-the-meaning-of-vegan
"Vegan Advocacy is the Only Solution," at
www.abolitionistapproach.com/vegan-advocacy-is-the-only-solution
"Is Veganism Elitist? No. But Nonveganism Is!," at
www.abolitionistapproach.com/veganism-elitist-no-nonveganism
Veganism, PETA, Farm Sanctuary, Peter Singer, 'Personal Purity,' and Principles of Justice," at
www.abolitionistapproach.com/veganism-peta-farm-sanctuary-peter-singer-personal-purity-principles-justice
"'But it took me 10 years to go vegan.' So What?," at
www.abolitionistapproach.com/took-10-years-go-vegan
"Commentary: Vegan Education/Advocacy, 'Forcing' Others to Go Vegan, and Animal Ethics as Involving Obligation and Not Choice, at
www.abolitionistapproach.com/commentary-vegan-educationadvocacy-

forcing-others-go-vegan-animal-ethics-involving-obligation-choice

"Creative, Non-Violent Vegan Education – Easy and Effective, at www.abolitionistapproach.com/creative-non-violent-vegan-education-easy-and-effective

"On 'Journeys,'" at www.abolitionistapproach.com/journeys

"The Problem With Single-Issue Campaigns and Why Veganism Must Be the Baseline," at www.abolitionistapproach.com/problem-with-single-issue-campaigns-and-why-veganism-must-be-the-baseline

"Veganism: Just Another Way of Reducing Suffering or a Fundamental Principle of Justice & Nonviolence?," at www.abolitionistapproach.com/veganism-just-another-way-of-reducing-suffering-or-a-fundamental-principle-of-justice-nonviolence

Additional Resources

www.HowDoIGoVegan.com

Principle Four

The Abolitionist Approach links the moral status of nonhumans with sentience alone and not with any other cognitive characteristic; all sentient beings are equal for the purpose of not being used exclusively as a resource.

Summary

Sentience is subjective awareness; there is some*one* who perceives and experiences the world. A sentient being has interests; that is, preferences, wants, or desires. If a being is sentient, then that is necessary and sufficient for the being to have the right not to be used as a means to human ends. The recognition of this right imposes on humans the moral obligation not to use that being as a resource. It is not necessary for a sentient being to have humanlike cognitive characteristics in order to be accorded the right not to be used as property.

Discussion

Rejecting the Foundation of Welfarism

In our discussion of *Principle Two,* we examined the welfarist position that animals do not have an interest in continuing to live (because they are supposedly not self-aware and so animal use does not per se raise a moral question) and that only issues of animal treatment matter. Animals don't know what they lose when we kill them, and as long as we provide them a reasonably pleasant life and a relatively pleasant death, we have discharged our moral obligations to them. The Abolitionist Approach rejects that position and maintains that any sentient being is, by virtue of being sentient, self-aware in the relevant sense for the purpose of having an interest in continued life, and that using and killing animals as human resources is unjust and morally indefensible however "humanely" animals are treated. The Abolitionist Approach maintains that all sentient beings have a moral right not to be used as replaceable resources; welfarists reject this idea.

As long as we buy into the notion that animals have to be self-aware in a humanlike way in order to have the right not to be used as resources for humans, we will continue to also embrace the idea that our use of animals who are not self-aware in a humanlike way does not per se raise a moral issue. We will continue to be stuck in the welfarist ideology that focuses on treatment and seeks to make animal exploitation more "humane." If we are ever going to challenge the idea that we can morally justify animal use (however "humane"), it is necessary that we recognize that humans and nonhumans are *equal* for the purpose of not being used as resources. That is, the Abolitionist Approach recognizes that all sentient beings have one fundamental, moral right: the right not to be used as property or exclusively as resources for others.

We recognize that all humans are holders of this moral right irrespective of their particular cognitive characteristics. That is, we do not promote the slavery of those who are not particularly intelligent or who are otherwise not cognitively similar to normal people. We may treat people differently based on their intelligence or other characteristics, but there is a basic minimum level of protection that we accord all humans—the right not to be used as the property of others. We do not do this where nonhumans are concerned. If we are ever going to be just in our treatment of nonhumans, we must reject the idea that animal use per se does not raise a moral issue. We must reject the idea that we do not have to accord animals a right not to be used because animals are sentient but are not self-aware in the same way humans are. Sentience must itself be sufficient—as it is in the case of humans—to provide the basis for the right not to be used as a resource.

The "Similar-Minds" Approach to Animal Ethics

In recent years, the welfarist movement has begun to promote the view that, if animals have a level of self-awareness that is more similar to humans, they should be regarded as having more moral value and entitled to a higher level of moral consideration and a higher level of protection than we accord to animals who are merely sentient.

There are many campaigns that focus on particular animals who are thought to be more "like us." These include nonhuman great apes, dolphins, whales, and elephants. The authors of this book have characterized this as the "similar-minds" approach to animal advocacy—that is, that those animals who are thought to be cognitively more like humans matter more morally and are entitled to greater protection.

The similar-minds approach, like the "happy exploitation" movement, can be traced to Peter Singer. In 1993, Singer co-edited a book of essays entitled *The Great Ape Project: Equality beyond Humanity,* which proposed that nonhuman great apes "have mental capacities and an emotional life sufficient to justify inclusion within the community of equals."[1] Singer argues that, because these nonhuman animals are genetically and cognitively similar to human animals, they deserve greater legal protection than other

---

[1]Paola Cavalieri and Peter Singer, eds., *The Great Ape Project: Equality beyond Humanity* (Fourth Estate 1993), 5.

nonhumans, who he, along with Bentham and others, believes live in "a kind of eternal present." This sort of approach to animal ethics is problematic because it *cannot* eliminate speciesist hierarchy; it can only redefine it. It will only result in creating new speciesist hierarchies in which we move some nonhumans, such as the great apes or dolphins, into a preferred group, and continue to treat all others as things lacking morally significant interests. So we can have campaigns involving "animal people" who care about nonhuman great apes or elephants but who are not vegan and eat cows, pigs, chickens, fishes, etc. Animals thought to be more cognitively similar to humans are accorded greater moral value and protection precisely *because* they are unlike all of the animals we routinely exploit, who remain on the other side of the person/thing divide. This leads Singer to make comments such as:

> You could say it's wrong to kill a being whenever a being is sentient or conscious. Then you would have to say it's just as wrong to kill a chicken or mouse as it is to kill you or me. I can't accept that idea. It may be just as wrong, but millions of chickens are killed every day. I can't think of that as a tragedy on the same scale as millions of humans being killed. What is different about humans? Humans are forward-looking beings, and they have hopes and desires for the future. That seems a plausible answer to the question of why it's so tragic when humans die.[2]

Singer's comments are problematic for several reasons. First, Singer assumes that chickens and other sentient nonhumans are not forward-looking beings. We have had little personal experience with chickens but we know enough about them to conclude that their behavior cannot be explained unless we attribute to them some sort of cognition that is equivalent to what we would characterize as forward-looking in humans. Chickens clearly have interests, preferences, and desires and are able to act to satisfy their interests and preferences. When we kill these nonhumans, we frustrate their ability to enjoy the satisfaction of their interests, preferences, and desires—just as we do when we kill humans.

We have had extensive experience with dogs and we can say quite confidently that we would be astonished if someone were to assert that dogs

---

[2] See http://archive.indystar.com/article/20090308/entertainment/903080313/Interview-Peter-Singer. This comment is discussed at http://www.abolitionistapproach.com/peter-singer-and-the-welfarist-position-on-the-lesser-value-of-nonhuman-life

are not forward-looking beings or that they do not have hopes and desires. We could offer many instances to the contrary. Here's one. One day, we went to the drive-through window at the bank. Our canine kids were with us. The teller put some small dog biscuits in the envelope with the deposit ticket. When we got home, we tossed the biscuits into the woods behind the house because the biscuits were not vegan and our dogs are. One of our dogs, Katie (who has since passed away at 21 years of age), saw us toss the biscuits. She kept looking at that area through the fence. Later in the day, as she was standing by the gate, we opened it to see if she would head in the direction of the biscuits. And she did. She ran straight to where the biscuits were. (We called her back and gave her vegan biscuits instead.) There is no other explanation for this behavior than that she had remembered we had thrown the biscuits into the woods and that she had spent several hours looking forward to getting them. To say that Katie was not thinking in a forward-looking way, or that she did not have preferences or desires in that situation (and in many others) is just false.

In any event, the underlying premise in Singer's position is that the only way to be forward looking, and to have hopes and desires, is to have them in the way that humans do. But that is clearly a speciesist position. Humans think in terms of concepts that are linked inextricably with symbolic communication—that is, language. The cognition of nonhumans is most likely very different from human cognition because nonhumans do not use symbolic communication. But that certainly does not mean that nonhumans do not have equivalent cognitive phenomena.

Second, and more important, is the moral value that Singer assigns to having the ability to plan for the future. What about humans who have amnesia and have a sense of themselves in the present but are unable to recall the past or plan for the future? Would killing them be morally wrong? Of course it would. Would we judge it as worse (morally or legally) to kill a person who did not have this condition? Of course not. We would regard both killings as equally culpable because in both cases we have deprived humans of their lives, which matter *to them*. The life of a hen is as valuable to her as our lives are to us, and as the life of the person with amnesia is to them.

Moreover, on Singer's analysis, the life of a human with more hopes and desires would be worth more than the life of a human who had fewer. So the life of a depressed person who may not be particularly excited about or able to plan for the future, or the life of a poor person whose hopes and desires are focused on the next meal or on a place to sleep for that night, is worth less than, say, the life of a Princeton professor like Singer who has lots and lots of hopes and plans for the future. That may be convenient for Singer but it is very unfair to the depressed or poor person.

Singer's comments reflect the welfarist notion that our use of animals is not the primary problem or even a moral problem at all because, as a factual matter, animals do not have an interest in their lives. That is, welfarists maintain that nonhumans have an interest in not suffering, but that, as they do not have an interest in continued life because they do not have hopes or future desires, we can use them for our purposes as long we treat them "humanely." Singer clearly accepts the welfarist principle that nonhumans are of less moral value than humans.

Third, this way of thinking sets up a standard that means that animals, however much they are "like us," can never win. For example, we have known for a long time that nonhuman great apes are very much like humans in all sorts of ways but we continue to exploit them. However much animals are like us, they are never enough like us to translate into an obligation on our part to stop exploiting them altogether. Indeed, Singer acknowledged that, in addition to nonhuman great apes, elephants, and dolphins, some birds and other animals appear to have mental continuity but, at least with respect to animals other than nonhuman great apes, he has thus far failed to recognize that this should establish a presumption against all use and killing. In our discussion of *Principle Two* we saw that, although Singer is a utilitarian who rejects moral rights for both nonhumans and humans, he recognizes a presumption in favor of not treating normal humans as replaceable resources. He appears to recognize this presumption as it applies to nonhuman great apes, but he does not recognize it with respect to other species that he regards as being more than sentient and as having mental continuity. The likely explanation for this failure is that Singer regards great apes as a group to have a relevantly similar level of mental continuity to that of normal humans, which would provide a direct reason not to use them as replaceable resources. The strength of the reason not to kill self-aware nonhuman animals "will vary with the degree to which the animal is capable of having desires for the future," and even if the animals we usually eat are self-aware, "they are still not self-aware to anything like the extent that humans normally are."[3] So even if animals are more like us, they are unlikely to be sufficiently like us so that they will receive rights or rights-type protection. Again, animals can never win.

The Elitism of the "Similar-Minds" Approach

The idea that animals must be cognitively like humans (beyond being sentient) to matter morally, or to matter enough not to be used exclusively as resources, is hopelessly elitist.

Assume we have two humans: a philosophy professor and a factory worker who has no higher education and has no interest in having any discussions that would be regarded by the philosopher as intellectually stimulating. If we were to say that it is better to be a philosophy professor dissatisfied than a factory worker satisfied, such an assertion would, quite rightly, be viewed as arbitrary and elitist. Although there is certainly a tradition in Western thought that assigns a higher value to intellectual pursuits than to other sorts of activities, that tradition was shaped almost exclusively by academics and others who valued intellectual pursuits and was not the result of any democratic or impartial assessment of competing pleasures. The notion that nonhuman animals have pains and pleasures that are different from, and lesser than, those of humans is no different from asserting that the pleasures and pains of a less intelligent or less educated human are inferior to those of a more intelligent or better educated one.

To the extent that humans and nonhumans have different sorts of minds, those differences may be relevant for some purposes, just as differences between and among humans may be relevant for some purposes. Mary's greater ability at math may justify our giving her a scholarship over Joe, who lacks ability at math. The rescued dogs who live with us very much like to sit with us when we watch movies, but we do not consider their likes and dislikes in movies when we choose what to watch because, at least as far as we can tell, they do not have any. So there are relevant differences between the minds of humans and the minds of nonhumans. Any differences, however, are not logically relevant to, for instance, the question whether we should

---

[3] Peter Singer, *Practical Ethics*, 3d ed. (Cambridge University Press 2011), 119, 122.

use dogs in painful experiments or kill them for other purposes, just as Joe's inability to do math is not relevant to the question whether we should take his kidney to save Mary or use him in an experiment to obtain data that may benefit Mary. We cannot claim that humans are superior based on their having more interests, or more intense interests, than nonhumans without begging the question and engaging in reasoning that, if applied in the human context, would quite rightly be seen as blatantly arbitrary and elitist.

The rights position, as we have developed it, rejects the notion that because some nonhumans, such as the nonhuman great apes, are more like humans, they are more deserving of moral status or legal protection than other animals. The fact that an animal is more cognitively similar to humans may be relevant to determining what other sorts of interests the animal has. But with respect to the animal's interest in her life and the harm that death constitutes to her, or with respect to her interest in not being made to experience pain and suffering, her being similar to humans is not relevant at all.

To be clear: if a being is sentient—that is, if they are perceptually aware—they have an interest in continuing to live and death is a harm to them. It is not necessary to have the autobiographical sense of self that we associate with normal adult humans. Moreover, we cannot say that their interest in their life or the quality of their pain or pleasure is of lesser moral value because their cognition is not the same as those of normal adult humans. The fact that the minds of humans differ from those of nonhumans does not mean that the life of a human has greater moral value any more than it means that the life of a human who has normal mental capacities has greater moral value than the life of a mentally disabled person or that the life of an intelligent person has greater moral value than the life of a less intelligent one. Although the differences between humans and animals may be important for some purposes, they are completely irrelevant to the immorality of using and killing animals, even if we do so "humanely."

Any attempt to justify our exploitation of nonhumans based on their lack of supposedly special human characteristics begs the moral question by assuming that certain characteristics are special and justify different treatment. Even if, for instance, humans were the only animals who can recognize themselves in mirrors or who can communicate through symbolic language, no human is capable of flying or breathing under water without assistance. What makes the ability to recognize oneself in a mirror or use symbolic language better in a moral sense than the ability to fly or breathe under water? The answer, of course, is that *we* say so and it is in our interest to say so.

Aside from self-interest, there is no reason to conclude that characteristics thought to be uniquely human have any value that allows us to use them as a non-arbitrary justification for exploiting nonhumans. Moreover, even if all nonhuman animals were to lack a particular characteristic beyond sentience, or to possess that characteristic to a lesser degree than humans, such a difference could not justify human exploitation of nonhumans.

Differences between humans and other animals may be relevant for other purposes. No sensible person argues that nonhuman animals should drive cars, vote, or attend universities, but such differences have no bearing on the question whether we should eat nonhumans or use them in experiments. We recognize this conclusion when it comes to humans. Whatever characteristic we identify as uniquely human will be seen to a lesser degree in some humans and not at all in others. Some humans will have the same deficiency that we attribute to nonhumans, and although the deficiency may be relevant for some purposes, it is not relevant to the question whether we should exploit such humans.

Ironically, those who promote a "some animals are better than other animals" approach are the very first to claim that promoting veganism as a moral baseline and treating all sentient beings as equals is "elitist." For example, Sea Shepherd is a charity that seeks to protect marine mammals, such as dolphins and whales. But the head of this charity, Paul Watson, claims that it is "elitist" to insist on veganism as a moral imperative. So Watson thinks that it's fine to ram a Japanese vessel in order to save a whale but that it is "purism" and "elitism" to insist that killing a chicken is as morally wrong as killing a whale. We disagree.

Sentience and Other Rights Approaches

The Abolitionist Approach is a rights theory that rejects the welfarist position. It is not the only rights approach that rejects animal welfare. But it is the *only* theory that requires sentience alone for full membership in the moral community and possession of the moral right not to be used exclusively as a resource. The theory articulated by Tom Regan in *The Case for Animal Rights* is both a rights theory and one that rejects the animal welfare approach. Regan maintains that we have no moral justification for treating animals exclusively as means to the ends of humans, so he does not rely on the supposed lesser moral value of nonhumans to justify animal use as Bentham and Singer do. The problem is that Regan's theory focuses on animals who have "preference autonomy," or who have interests and are capable of acting in ways to satisfy those interests. He says that although other animals may not have this characteristic, mammals aged one year or more certainly do. Although Regan is open to other animals having moral status, his theory is limited by the requirement that animals have preference autonomy. The Abolitionist Approach rejects this limitation and maintains that no characteristic other than sentience is necessary for an animal to hold the moral right not to be used as a replaceable resource.

Moreover, Regan argues that in a situation in which there is an "exceptional" conflict, such as a situation in which we are in a lifeboat and must choose whether to save a dog or a human, we should choose to save the life of the human over the dog because death is a greater harm for the human. According to Regan, "the harm that death is, is a function of the opportunities for satisfaction it forecloses," and death for an animal, "though a harm, is not comparable to the harm that death would be" for humans.[4] Indeed, Regan says that we would be obligated to sacrifice any number of dogs (or other animals) if that were necessary to save a human life. This rests on what we believe is a speciesist view of animal cognition. We do not think that there is any reason whatsoever to believe that a nonhuman has fewer opportunities for satisfaction than does a human and that, as a result, death is a lesser harm for a nonhuman. We certainly do not think that we are morally obligated to kill a million dogs, as Regan maintains, to save a human in a situation of

---

[4]Tom Regan, *The Case for Animal Rights* (University of California Press 1983), 324.

conflict, however exceptional.

Although there are other differences between the Abolitionist Approach and Regan's position, the difference between the abolitionist position and Regan's position on the issue of sentience is key.

Conclusion

If we want to think seriously about the human/nonhuman relationship, we need to focus on one, and only one, characteristic: sentience. If an animal is sentient, or subjectively aware, irrespective of any other characteristic that animal may have, we must recognize that animal as the holder of a right not to be used exclusively as a resource for others.

Further Reading

Books

Gary L. Francione and Robert Garner, *The Animal Rights Debate: Abolition or Regulation?* (Columbia University Press 2010), 14-24.'

Gary L. Francione, *Introduction to Animal Rights: Your Child or the Dog?* (Temple University Press 2000).

Essays

Gary L. Francione, "Taking Sentience Seriously," *Journal of Animal Law and Ethics,* vol. 1, 1-18 (2006) and reprinted in Gary L. Francione, *Animals as Persons: Essays in the Abolition of Animal Exploitation* (Columbia University Press, 2008) 129-147.

Gary L. Francione, "Our Hypocrisy," *New Scientist,* June 4, 2005, available at www.abolitionistapproach.com/media/links/p8/similar-minds.pdf

Blog Posts

"Sentience and Personhood," at
www.abolitionistapproach.com/sentience-and-personhood

"Only Sentience Matters," at
www.abolitionistapproach.com/only-sentience-matters

"Sentience," at
www.abolitionistapproach.com/sentience

"The Great Ape Project: Not So Great," at
www.abolitionistapproach.com/the-great-ape-project-not-so-great

Principle Five

Abolitionists reject all forms of human discrimination, including racism, sexism, heterosexism, ageism, ableism, and classism—just as they reject speciesism.

Summary

The Abolitionist Approach to Animal Rights rejects speciesism because, like racism, sexism, heterosexism, and other forms of human discrimination, it uses a morally irrelevant criterion (species) to discount and devalue the interests of sentient beings. But any opposition to speciesism makes sense *only* as part of a general opposition to all forms of discrimination. That is, we *cannot* oppose speciesism but claim that, as animal advocates, we do not have a position on these other forms of discrimination. We cannot say that we reject species as a morally objectionable criterion to discount or devalue the interests of nonhumans but that we do not have a position on whether race, sex, or sexual orientation/preference are morally objectionable criteria when used to discount or devalue human interests. Our opposition to speciesism *requires* that we oppose *all* discrimination.

Discussion

All Discrimination is Similar

The world of morality is binary. There are *persons* (those beings who have moral value and to whom we have moral obligations) and *things* (which do not have moral value and to which we can have no moral obligations). To say that a being has moral value is simply to say that the being is someone to whom we have moral obligations. Human chattel slavery is particularly objectionable because it involves treating humans as things—as property—that have no inherent value and only have value as commodities that are bought and sold. To say that a being has inherent value is simply to say that they value their interests even if no one else does. Slavery "otherizes" those who are enslaved. That is, although they ought to be treated as persons, they are placed on the thing side of the person/thing distinction. And there neither is, nor can there be, a morally sound reason for this placement. In the case of slavery in the United States, slavery was based on race, and race is an irrelevant criterion.

Speciesism is morally objectionable because, like the racism that was used to justify human slavery, it allows us to place nonhuman animals on the thing side of the person/thing distinction and treat them as property based solely on species. Species, like race, is an irrelevant criterion insofar as determining moral value is concerned.

Treating beings—human or nonhuman—as property is particularly odious because it denies those beings any moral value whatsoever. But there are other forms of discrimination that, while not denying personhood to beings, devalue certain interests that they have based on irrelevant criteria. For example, we no longer have race-based human chattel slavery as an institutional matter (although human slavery still exists in the world). But we do have racism, which involves devaluing the interests of persons based solely on race. That is, we no longer enslave people of color and buy and sell them, but there are still many instances in which the interests of persons of color are devalued solely on the basis of race. Because our culture is patriarchal, we devalue the interests of women based solely on their biological sex. Because our culture is homophobic and heteronormative, we devalue the interests of persons who are homosexual or who are transgender. Because we worship materialism, we often devalue the interests of those who are in lower socioeconomic classes.

In all of these cases, we violate the fundamental moral rule that we encountered in the discussion of *Principle One*—we fail to treat similar cases in a similar way. Although devaluing the interests of a person of color based solely on race is different from treating a person of color as a non-person and as a chattel slave also because of race, *all* discrimination involves failing to treat similar cases in a similar way. All discrimination involves otherizing in that the victim of discrimination is treated as the "other," whether as the non-person other who is treated as property or as the person whose interests are devalued, based solely on irrelevant criteria.

As we saw in our earlier discussions, Peter Singer, who claims to reject speciesism, is very much guilty of speciesism. Singer says that we should accord similar weight to the interests of humans and nonhumans. But he thinks that most animals have no (or qualitatively less) interest in not being used and killed and that they only have an interest in not suffering. This leads him to accept using nonhumans as replaceable resources even though he has a presumption against such use where normal humans are concerned. The presumption functions like a right but, as Singer is a utilitarian who rejects moral rights, it may be rebutted if the consequences of doing so militate in that direction. So Singer would say that he is not being a speciesist because most nonhuman animals do not have an interest in not being used as replaceable resources and, therefore, not according protection against this use (as he does with humans) is not speciesism. He would claim he's not treating similar interests in a dissimilar way because animals do not have that particular interest in the first place.

We saw earlier that such an analysis assumes that it is only humanlike self-awareness that counts for purposes of giving rise to an interest in continued existence, and that assumption is completely arbitrary. Moreover, it leads him to maintain that animals who are property can be treated as less morally significant beings; that is, Singer strongly promotes the animal welfare paradigm, which, as we saw earlier, is morally problematic and unworkable as a practical matter because animals are property.

In any event, the Abolitionist Approach rejects speciesism because it excludes animals from the moral community by allowing their use as replaceable resources. But, because any ethical theory to be plausible must be consistent, the Abolitionist Approach rejects *all* forms of discrimination.

Some animal advocates claim that the animal rights movement ought to focus only on animals and should not take a position on issues of human discrimination. The Abolitionist Approach rejects that position. It makes no sense to say that we are opposed to otherizing nonhumans based on the irrelevant criterion of species but that we are not opposed to the otherizing of humans based on the irrelevant criteria of race, sex, sexual orientation/preference, gender, class, or ability.

The Use of Human Discrimination Supposedly to Promote Animal Rights

To say that abolitionists reject all discrimination—whether against nonhumans or humans—is not to say that abolitionists have to stop their work for animals and do human rights work instead. It is to say that abolitionists should see issues of human rights and animal rights as inextricably intertwined and should not engage in or support human discrimination. And they should certainly never promote human discrimination supposedly to promote animal matters.

Unfortunately, because many advocates have seen issues of animal ethics and ethics involving humans as mutually exclusive, there has been a tendency to promote campaigns that otherize humans. Nowhere has this been more apparent than in the overtly sexist and misogynistic campaigns that have become the trademark of People for the Ethical Treatment of Animals (PETA) and have, to a lesser degree, been adopted by other animal advocacy organizations. PETA launched these campaigns in 1989 or so, starting with scantily clad or naked women who said they would rather "go naked than wear fur." In the following years, these campaigns became more and more explicit; for example, they have included depictions of women masturbating with vegetables and women involved in various sadomasochistic scenes. Additionally, PETA also had "State of the Union Undress" videos that featured women who stripped naked while talking about PETA's supposed accomplishments of the past year. As the women removed their clothing, clips of the United States Congress clapping enthusiastically were spliced in.

Abolitionists do not support such campaigns and, indeed, explicitly reject them. Campaigns that commodify women have no place in an ethical approach that rejects the commodification of nonhumans. The fact that the women who appear in these campaigns do so voluntarily does not, despite PETA's claim, mean that the campaigns are not sexist or misogynistic. The point is not that women should not have the right to do what they want with their bodies—including engaging in commodifying themselves. Women have the right to choose how to use their bodies. The point is that the choice that women make to participate in these campaigns is a choice that is made in the context of a patriarchal culture, and that these campaigns commodify women. Indeed, the very point of these campaigns is to capitalize on that commodification.

Not only is the sexism and misogyny of these campaigns inherently immoral, but, as a practical matter, perpetuating the commodification of women will do *nothing* to change social thinking about the commodification of nonhumans. PETA and other animal organizations have been using sexism and misogyny in their anti-fur campaigns for years. And what result has it had? The fur industry is stronger now than it has ever been. Many of the celebrities who once went naked for PETA are wearing fur again. We have yet to meet a single person who was moved to consider the animal issue because they saw a naked woman sitting in a cage.

The bottom line is clear: in addition to the moral issues involved in sexism and misogyny, the practical reality is that as long as we treat women like meat, we will continue to treat animals like meat.

In fact, it is no surprise that the ideology of postmodern feminism, which supports the "happy" commodification of women under the pretense of their being "empowered" by it, is similar to the ideology of new welfarism in its "happy" exploitation of nonhumans. Both ideologies keep the status quo of the oppression of women and nonhumans in place. New welfarism reinforces the default position of animals as property and postmodern feminism reinforces the default position of women as sexual objects. They both just put smiley faces on what is in essence a very reactionary message.

In sum, as long as we tolerate racism, sexism, heterosexism, and other forms of discrimination, there will be speciesism. That is one reason why it is important that animal advocates should never think of themselves as "one issue" people. Speciesism is morally objectionable because, like racism, sexism, and other forms of discrimination, it excludes beings from the scope of moral concern on the basis of an irrelevant criterion. It makes no difference whether that irrelevant criterion is race, sex, sexual orientation, or species. We cannot sensibly say that we oppose speciesism but that we support, or have no position on, other forms of discrimination. We oppose speciesism because it is like racism, sexism, and other forms of discrimination. Our opposition to speciesism logically implies a rejection of these other forms of discrimination.

Again, this does not mean that animal advocates must stop their work on behalf of animals and become human rights advocates instead. It does, however, mean that they should always make clear to others that they, as animal advocates, oppose all forms of discrimination and that no one should ever practice discrimination in their own lives.

But What About Human Problems? Don't They Come First?

Animal advocates frequently hear such things as:

"There are too many human problems in the world that we have to solve first before we think about animals."

"Let's work on world peace first; we can then work on animal rights."

No one is saying that those who campaign for human rights should stop doing so and should instead campaign for animal rights. Rather, the point is that if we accept that animals are members of the moral community, we should stop eating, wearing, or consuming animals in our individual lives. Becoming a vegan does not require that you stop advocating for abused children, battered women, or against war.

We encourage those who are engaged in the struggle for human rights and social justice to continue in those struggles. We commend and support them; we have worked for human rights throughout our legal careers. We simply urge them to stop consuming animals as food, wearing them, using products that contain them, or patronizing any form of entertainment that uses animals. To put it another way—everyone has to eat, wear clothing, and use other products, whether they are working for social justice for women or children, campaigning against war, or doing anything else. If someone working on a human rights issue never did anything else on the animal issue, their act of going vegan, and the example that they would set for friends and family, would themselves constitute important forms of activism that would in no way interfere with their work for women or children, or against war. Becoming an advocate for abolition is something that you can do at your next meal or next time you shop for clothing and other products.

It is a mistake to see issues of human and animal exploitation as mutually exclusive. On the contrary, all exploitation is inextricably intertwined. All exploitation is a manifestation of violence. All discrimination is a manifestation of violence. As long as we tolerate violence of any sort, there will be violence of every sort. As Russian novelist Leo Tolstoy noted, "As long as there are slaughterhouses, there will be battlefields." As long as humans regard it as normal to slaughter animals for food for which there is no justification other than the trivial pleasure we get from eating animals, they will regard it just as normal to use violence when they think that something more important is at stake.

Many altruistic people admirably want to change the world but do not see that the most important change comes at the level of the individual. As Mahatma Gandhi said, "You must be the change you want to see in the world." Veganism is an important element of a nonviolent life as there can be no doubt that all animal foods and animal products are the result of violence.

If you want a nonviolent world, you must embrace nonviolence in your own life.

Conclusion

All forms of discrimination, including but not limited to speciesism, involve treating some group of beings as *others,* and then proceeding to deny these others full membership in the moral community. In extreme cases, this otherization may involve a complete denial of moral personhood and a treatment of the others as things who are excluded entirely from the moral community. Human slavery and the treatment of animals as property are examples of this complete exclusion.

The Abolitionist Approach rejects *all* otherization. Speciesism is morally wrong because it is like racism, sexism, heterosexism, cissexism, classism, ableism, etc. And just as we reject speciesism, we are committed to rejecting all of these other forms of discrimination as well.

Further Reading

Books

Gary L. Francione and Robert Garner, *The Animal Rights Debate: Abolition or Regulation?* (Columbia University Press 2010), 83-84.

Gary L. Francione, *Rain Without Thunder: The Ideology of the Animal Rights Movement* (Temple University Press 1996), 74-76.

Blog Posts

"Social Justice, Human Rights, and Being Vegan," at www.abolitionistapproach.com/social-justice-human-rights-and-being-vegan

"Human and Nonhuman Rights as Inextricably Intertwined: In a Nutshell," at www.abolitionistapproach.com/human-and-nonhuman-rights-as-inextricably-intertwined-in-a-nutshell

"Human Rights and Animal Rights: Perfect Together," at www.abolitionistapproach.com/human-rights-and-animal-rights-perfect-together

"Commentary #9: Using Sexism to Promote Animal Rights," at www.abolitionistapproach.com/commentary-using-sexism-to-promote-animal-rights

"Sexism and Misogyny in the Movement," at www.abolitionistapproach.com/sexism-and-misogyny-in-the-movement

"Happy Meat and Sexism," at www.abolitionistapproach.com/happy-meat-and-sexism

"Postmodern Feminism and Animal Welfare: Perfect Together," at www.abolitionistapproach.com/postmodern-feminism-and-animal-welfare-perfect-together

Principle Six

Abolitionists recognize the principle of nonviolence as a core principle of the animal rights movement.

Summary

The Abolitionist Approach promotes nonviolence because it sees the animal rights movement as an extension of the peace movement to include concerns about nonhuman animals. Moreover, given that most people engage in animal exploitation, there is no principled way to distinguish exploiters for the purpose of justifying violence. Finally, because there is pervasive exploitation, violence cannot be understood as anything but a pathological reaction to what is regarded as normal. The only real option is, on the individual level, to embrace veganism as a moral baseline and, on the social level, to engage in creative, nonviolent vegan education from an abolitionist perspective.

Discussion

The Three Problems with Violence

The Abolitionist Approach opposes violence for three reasons.

First, the animal rights position is the ultimate affirmation of peace, and, therefore, the ultimate rejection of violence. The peace movement seeks to end conflict between and among humans. The Abolitionist Approach maintains that that the animal rights movement should embrace that goal and extend it to end conflict between humans and nonhumans. The animal rights movement should be the non-speciesist peace movement.

The reason that we are in our current global mess is that throughout history, we have engaged and continue to engage in violent actions that we have sought to justify as an undesirable means to a desirable end. Anyone who has ever used violence claims to regret having resorted to it, but argues that some desirable goal supposedly justified its use. The problem is that this facilitates an endless cycle of violence where anyone who feels strongly about something can engage in violence toward others as a means to achieving the greater good and those who are the targets of that violence may find a justification for their violent response. So on and on it goes.

This is consequentialist moral thinking and it is destroying the world as well as leading to some very peculiar contradictions. Much of the West claims to embrace Christianity. However unclear on some issues the New Testament may be, it is certainly clear that violence is to be rejected. Nevertheless, Christian leaders and their Christian electorates justify the most violent of actions with professed great reluctance in order to achieve a supposed greater good, whatever it may be. Those against whom these violent actions are directed also claim to adhere to religions that reject violence, but feel justified in using violence in response. So we have people, all of who claim to reject violence as a fundamental religious matter, engaging in violence.

And we say that humans are rational and nonhumans are not.

Violence treats others as means to ends rather than as ends in themselves. When we engage in violence against others—whether they are human or nonhuman—we ignore their inherent value. We treat them only as *things* that have no value except that which we decide to give them. This is what leads people to engage in crimes of violence against people of color, women, homosexuals, transpersons, etc. It is what leads us to commodify nonhumans and treat them as resources that exist solely for our use. All of it is wrong and should be rejected.

Second, there is no coherent way to identify legitimate targets for violence. If it is, as some claim, morally acceptable to use violence against animal exploiters, exactly against whom is this violence to be directed? The farmer raises animals because most humans demand to eat meat and other animal products. The farmer raises those animals in intensive conditions because consumers want animal products to be as inexpensive as possible. These institutional exploiters do what they do because the rest of us demand that they do so. If we stopped demanding animal products, the producers of those products would put their capital into other activities. Although government and industry currently help to create and support the demand for animal products, through subsidies and advertising, we can choose to ignore their encouragement. As a political matter, we can reject governmental policies that support animal products. If a sufficient number of people became vegan, the incentive for governmental support for animal use would diminish. So the responsibility for animal exploitation rests primarily on those who demand animal products. This includes all of those "conscientious omnivores" or nonvegan animal advocates who consume "happy" animal products. It is easier to characterize farmers as the "enemy," but that ignores the reality of the situation.

What about the vivisector, a common target of those who advocate violence? Putting aside the debate about whether vivisection actually produces data useful to address problems of human health, most of the illnesses for which vivisectors are using animals are conditions that could be avoided entirely or drastically reduced if humans would stop eating animal foods and engaging in such destructive behaviors as smoking, excessive alcohol consumption, drug use, and a failure to exercise. Again, who is the real culprit? We certainly do not think that vivisection is justifiable for any reason, but we find it curious that those who advocate violence can see vivisectors as detached from the social conditions that give rise to vivisection. In these conditions we are *all* complicit.

Moreover, we must not forget that there are always multiple ways of addressing health problems. Vivisection is one way, and, in the view of many (including us), it is not a particularly effective choice. The decision to invest social resources into vivisection rather than in other, arguably far more effective, ways reflects a political decision as much as, and probably more than, a scientific one. For example, the considerable expenditure on AIDS research using animals has produced little of use to humans suffering from AIDS, and most of what has resulted in longer and better lives for those suffering from HIV and AIDS has come from clinical trials with humans who have consented to those trials. It is certainly plausible that if the money spent on animal research were instead spent on public safe-sex education campaigns, needle exchanges, and condom distribution, the rate of new HIV cases would drop dramatically. The choice to use animal experiments to address the problem is, in many ways, a political and social decision. Animal experiments are considered to be an acceptable way of solving the AIDS problem, whereas needle exchanges, condom distribution, and safe-sex education are politically controversial. So again, the vivisector is not the only culprit here. Indeed, it may well be argued that those primarily responsible for the use of animals in AIDS research are the reactionary politicians who respond to a reactionary political base that rejects more effective ways of dealing with AIDS.

Gary Francione had the following (approximated) discussion with someone who was promoting violence at a lecture he was giving at a university:

"If a vivisector is using 60 dogs per year in painful experiments, do you not think that it is justifiable to use violence against that person?"

"Let me ask you: is your mother a vegan?"

"What's that got to do with it?"

"Is she?"

"No. She's not."

"What animal products does she consume?"

"She does not eat beef but she does eat chicken and fish."

"Does she eat these often?"

"Yes."

"Your mother is responsible for many more deaths per year than is the vivisector (not taking into account whether the vivisector is or is not a vegan). Is it morally justifiable to use violence against your mother?"

"It's not the same thing."

"Really? What's the difference?"

Francione got no answer because there was no good answer to give.

Third, it is not clear to us what those who support violence hope to achieve as a practical matter. They certainly are not causing the public to become more sympathetic to the plight of nonhuman animals. If anything, the contrary is true and these actions have a most negative effect in terms of public perception. We live in a world where virtually anyone who can afford to eat animal products does so. In such a world, there is no context in which such violence can be interpreted in any way other than as negative.

In other words, when eating animal products is considered by most people as "natural" or "normal" as drinking water or breathing air, violence is quite likely to be seen as something morally abhorrent and will do nothing to further progressive thinking about the issue of animal exploitation.

Animal exploitation is pervasive in our society. This is the case because we think that the ends (the supposed benefits we derive from animal use) justify the means (imposing suffering and death on billions of nonhumans every year), and because we treat animals exclusively as commodities and ignore their inherent value. This situation cannot be meaningfully addressed by applying these notions to justify violence toward humans.

The fact that at least some so-called animal advocates who endorse violence are not even vegan is truly bewildering. These people care so much about animals that they advocate inflicting harm on other humans who exploit nonhumans but cannot seem to stop exploiting nonhumans themselves.

Animal Welfare Reform and Violence

There is a sense in which the welfarist position and the pro-violence position are theoretically similar. Welfarists characterize institutional users as the primary problem and focus their attention on getting these users to reform their practices. However, institutional users are economic actors who will do what they regard as efficient; they will make changes that increase production efficiency, and they will cater to niche markets, but they are not going to be the catalyst in widespread institutional change. Those who support violence similarly focus on the institutional exploiter and fail to recognize that, as long as there is ubiquitous demand for animal products and no acceptance of the moral personhood of nonhumans, violence will do nothing as a practical matter. If you destroy five slaughterhouses and the demand for meat remains the same, new slaughterhouses will be built (or existing ones expanded). If you shut down a company that supplies animals used in vivisection but the demand for animals remains the same because the public supports vivisection, someone else will supply those animals. The only way that animal use will stop or be reduced significantly is if the paradigm shifts and demand drops.

The Abolitionist Approach: Passive?

This is not to say that the Abolitionist Approach advocates a passive approach to animal ethics. On the contrary: going vegan based on the recognition that veganism is a moral imperative, and not just a matter of reducing suffering or an occasional lifestyle choice, is a nonviolent act of defiance. It is a refusal to participate in the injustice of exploiting innocent and vulnerable beings. Embracing abolitionist veganism represents your public statement that you will no longer participate in the exploitation of the vulnerable and your public withdrawal from institutionalized speciesism. Going vegan from a recognition of the inherent value of nonhuman animals is the most important action you can undertake as an individual.

The next most important thing you can do is to educate others about abolitionist veganism. There are those who claim that creative, nonviolent vegan education, which is what we propose in order to shift the moral paradigm, is insufficient because that approach will not work fast enough given the severity of the problem and the various social, political, economic, and ecological consequences of animal exploitation.

We do not doubt that animal use is nothing short of a disaster in every respect and that it is the most significant contributing factor to the overall peril of our planet. But it is beyond pure fantasy to believe that violence, even if it were morally justifiable, which we maintain it is not, would be the solution that would move things along faster and address this admittedly alarming situation in an effective way.

As we mentioned above, most humans see animal use as the default, "normal" position. Acts of violence *cannot* be seen as anything other than attacks on conduct that is regarded by most people as entirely unobjectionable and morally acceptable (at least as long as it is "humane").

Engaging in violence, which will necessarily be interpreted by most people as pathological, is not going to cause people to think that animal use is objectionable; if anything, violence will serve the ends of those who want to portray any effort to shift the paradigm—including peaceful and nonviolent efforts—as part of an overall pathological and objectionable ethic. Promoting violence is not only inconsistent with the ethic of peace; it will serve to frustrate its acceptance.

So what is the answer? As we said in our discussion of *Principle Three,* creative, nonviolent, vegan education is the answer. Abolitionist vegan education can take many forms. The only limit is that these efforts be nonviolent, and they should obviously be creative so that they can engage people. This education, like all education seeking to effect truly radical change, is very hard work. But, unlike the alternatives, it is the *only* option that will shift the paradigm and result in a fundamentally different way of assessing the underlying moral issue.

The Impossibility of Avoiding Harm

A frequent comment that we hear is, "But even if I go vegan, I will not be able to avoid all harm to animals as there are animal by-products in just about everything and animals are killed in crop production." This is an important comment to address and with which to end this book, as it allows us to make a broader statement about nonviolence.

Yes, there are animal by-products in many things, our world is literally built with the bodies of animals. And the reason that animal by-products are ubiquitous is that we kill billions of animals and, therefore, slaughterhouse by-products are cheap and easily available. If we lived in a vegan world, those by-products would not be available and other non-animal substances would be used instead.

Yes, animals are killed in crop production but many fewer animals would be killed if we ate plants directly instead of feeding them to animals whom we eat. If we all ate plants, there would be many fewer acres under cultivation because it takes many pounds of plants to produce one pound of animal products. And if we were all abolitionist vegans, we have no doubt that we would all be a great deal more concerned about those incidental and unintended deaths.

But this sort of comment about the inability to avoid all harm requires that we recognize an indisputable fact: our actions have negative impacts on others—human and nonhuman. Indeed, as adherents of Jainism, a spiritual tradition that began in India, recognize as a central tenet of their tradition, which is organized around the principle of *ahimsa,* or nonviolence: life in the material world necessarily involves our harming other beings. This is clearly true. For example, however little we consume, we all consume products and producing these involves incidental harm to humans and nonhumans. Even if we buy vegan fair-trade clothing, that clothing is made by humans, some of whom will inevitably be physically injured in the production process regardless of whether or not they are making a fair wage. Some nonhumans will also inevitably be injured by some aspect of the manufacturing process.

Of course, the inevitability of unintended or incidental harm does not mean that there is no moral difference between that harm and intended or deliberate harm. For example, when we build a road, we know that people will be killed and injured in accidents on that road. But that does not mean that there is no difference between building a road and deliberately killing the number of people likely to be killed on that road. Critics of veganism who make the argument that vegans cannot avoid all unintended or unintentional harm are saying, in essence, that if we cannot avoid all harm, we should not eliminate the harm over which we have control. If we cannot stop all traffic deaths, then murder is morally acceptable. This is obviously a position that no one would accept in the human context.

The Abolitionist Approach does not maintain that we can avoid all harm to nonhuman animals. We clearly can't. What we *can* do is not participate directly in harming animals and withdraw from the institutionalized exploitation of animals. We can refuse to treat sentient nonhumans as property, as things that exist exclusively as resources for humans.

However, even if we all went vegan and embraced a nonviolent ethic, some humans and animals would still be harmed as an indirect result of our actions, but there would be many fewer instances of harm. Any harm must be taken seriously, even if it does not rise to the moral level of deliberate or intentional harm. A vegan world would inevitably devise more creative solutions to mitigate that harm. Right now, a big part of the problem is that, although many people claim to embrace nonviolence as a guiding moral or spiritual principle, few think very much about how that principle should guide their day-to-day activity. The situation would be very different in a vegan world.

Those of us concerned about nonviolence are obligated to go vegan. We can build on that veganism as the moral baseline and seek always to act in a careful and non-negligent way so that we do not incidentally harm animals. For example, we should drive as little as practicable and, when we do drive, we should always do so carefully so that we do not accidentally harm animals (or humans for that matter). We should all be mindful about consumption and seek to consume as little as possible. The next time you want to buy something, ask yourself, "Do I really need that?" We should recognize that the heavier our footprint on the earth, the more harm that we incidentally and unintentionally inflict on humans and nonhumans alike. But if we went vegan and approached all of our conduct with nonviolence in mind, we would do a great deal better than we have done in the past and are doing now.

A world in which we all consumed plants and no animals were harmed for human purposes would be a world in which we would all be healthier— morally, physically, and spiritually.

Conclusion

The bottom line is clear. The only way that we are ever going to have a significant impact on the problem of animal use is through education. That starts with our becoming vegans and rejecting violence against animals in our own lives, and spreads through creative, nonviolent vegan education. Unlike the alternatives, abolitionist vegan education *will* bring about a revolution—of the heart.

In the end, those are the only revolutions that succeed.

Further Reading

Books

Gary L. Francione and Robert Garner, *The Animal Rights Debate: Abolition or Regulation?* (Columbia University Press 2010), 80-83.

Blog Posts

"On Violence," at
www.abolitionistapproach.com/on-violence

"Commentary #5: On Violence," at
www.abolitionistapproach.com/a-commentary-on-violence

"On Vivisection and Violence," at
www.abolitionistapproach.com/on-vivisection-and-violence

"More on Violence and Animal Rights," at
www.abolitionistapproach.com/more-on-violence-and-animal-rights

"A Comment on Violence," at
www.abolitionistapproach.com/a-comment-on-violence

A Note About the Abolitionist Approach, Morality, Religion, and Spirituality

In order to embrace the Abolitionist Approach to Animal Rights, it is not necessary to be spiritual or religious, or to be an atheist. You can be a spiritual or religious person, or you can be an atheist, or anything in between. It does not matter.

This is what does matter:

(1) You have moral concern about animals and you *want* to do right by animals. That moral concern/moral impulse can come from *any* source, spiritual/religious or non-spiritual/non-religious; and

(2) You regard as valid the logical arguments that our moral concern should not be limited to some nonhumans, but should extend to all sentient beings, and that we should abolish, and not regulate, animal exploitation.

This topic comes up often and we provide the following essay written by Gary Francione in 2012 and posted on www.AbolitionistApproach.com.

Moral Concern, Moral Impulse, and Logical Argument in Animal Rights Advocacy

Anyone who has ever done animal advocacy has had the experience of explaining rationally why animal exploitation can't be morally justified, only to have the person with whom they are talking say something like, "Yes, that's interesting but I just don't think that it's wrong to eat animal products," or "I think you're being perfectly logical but I just love ice cream and cheese and am going to continue eating them."

How can this be? How can people reject logical and rational arguments?

The answer is simple: logic and rationality are crucial to moral analysis. But they can't tell us the whole story about moral reasoning. It's more complicated than logical syllogisms. Moral reasoning—about animals or anything else—requires something more than logic. That something else involves two closely related but conceptually distinct notions: *moral concern* and *moral impulse,* which precede our engagement on a rational or logical level.

To put this in the context of animal ethics, in order to accept an argument that leads to the conclusion that all sentient beings are full members of the moral community and that we should abolish, and not regulate, animal exploitation, you must care morally about animals. You do not necessarily have to "like" or "love" animals. You do not have to have a house full of rescued animals or even have one rescued animal. But you have to accept that at least some animals are members of the moral community; that they are nonhuman moral persons to whom we have direct moral obligations.

And you have to *want* to act morally with respect to animals; you have to have a moral impulse concerning animals. You have to *feel* your moral beliefs in the sense that you want to do the right thing by animals. If you do, logic and rationality can be used to make compelling arguments that all sentient beings have that moral status and that no animal exploitation can be morally justified.

But if you don't care about animals morally and you don't want to do right by them, then all of the arguments in the world won't make much difference. If you do not think we owe animals *anything,* you won't be very interested in arguments that concern which animals we have direct moral obligations to, or what those obligations require us to do.

Logic and Rationality: Necessary but not Sufficient

In my book *Introduction to Animal Rights: Your Child or the Dog?,* I make a number of arguments based on logic and rationality. Here is just one:

1. The imposition of suffering on any sentient being requires an adequate moral justification and pleasure, amusement, or convenience cannot suffice as adequate to justify imposing suffering on any sentient being.

2. The most "humane" animal agriculture involves considerable suffering imposed on sentient beings.

3. As a general matter, our best (and only) justification for eating animal products is pleasure, amusement, or convenience.

4. Therefore, we cannot morally justify eating animal products.

This is all very logical. But the argument is not going to go anywhere if you don't accept the first premise and want to act on it. If you do not accept that you have any obligation to justify in a meaningful way the harm you impose on animals, we can't even get started talking about animal ethics. Logic and rationality can help us to ascertain what we owe nonhuman moral persons but logic and rationality are useless in the face of someone who just does not care morally about animals and who rejects the notion that any justification for the imposition of harm is required.

Science is also useless where the first premise is concerned. There is no way to prove "scientifically" that we have an obligation to justify the imposition of harm on a sentient being. As any first-year philosophy student knows, you cannot derive an "ought" from an "is."

So why should we accept the first premise?

I maintain that the first principle is self-evidently true. All sentient beings matter morally and before I adversely affect the interests of any sentient being, I am obliged to justify my action. When I use "true" here, I mean it in the same sense that I mean it when I say that the cup on my desk is red. The statement, "The cup is red" expresses a true proposition. The cup on my desk *is* red. Similarly, the statement, "We need to have a morally sufficient justification for imposing suffering on any sentient being" expresses a true proposition that reflects our moral intuition that suffering is bad.

The proposition expressed in the statement, "And a sufficient justification must exclude pleasure, amusement, or convenience," which could also be a separate premise, is also self-evidently true because if a sufficient justification could encompass such reasons, then nothing would be excluded by the principle. Think about it: to say, "We need a sufficient justification to harm a child but it is okay to hurt a child for no reason other than we want to" would render the principle requiring the justification of harm completely meaningless.

If someone were to ask me to prove the first premise with a scientific experiment or in some other way that would satisfy a strict empiricist, I could not do that. But so what? That does not mean the propositions expressed in the first premise are not true. Could someone deny the truth of the first premise? Sure they could. But someone could also deny the truth of the proposition concerning my red cup. We can be skeptics when it comes to moral principles, but we can be skeptics about anything. Who knows whether the cup is red? I may be hallucinating. I may not exist in the way that I think I do. I may be nothing more than a brain in a jar being stimulated by electrodes to have the experience of seeing a red cup, which does not exist at all.

I do not think that there is anything controversial in saying that the first premise is self-evidently true. I would posit that most people, when asked to think about it, would agree with the self-evidently true status of the first premise. Indeed, the theme of *Introduction to Animal Rights* is that we do claim to agree with the first premise but we fail to think rationally about what that moral rule means. That is, the problem is not that we cannot prove the first premise rationally; the problem is that although we claim to accept the moral truth of the principle, we either do not have the moral impulse to want to follow through with what we say we believe (and, as I explain below, I think that's another way of saying we don't really have moral concern) or we don't think rationally about what that principle requires us to do in terms of practical action.

Simon the Sadist and Michael Vick

In *Introduction to Animal Rights*, I introduced the character of Simon the Sadist, who derived pleasure from blowtorching dogs. We would all regard such conduct as monstrous. The point of Simon as a character was to demonstrate that Simon's conduct violates the principle that we all accept: that imposing suffering on a sentient being requires an adequate moral justification and Simon's pleasure does not constitute an adequate moral justification. The rest of the book argued that our acceptance of this moral principle required that we regard all sentient beings, and not just dogs, as members of the moral community, and that we abolish all animal exploitation.

More recently, I have made the same points in the context of actual instances of harming animals, such as the matter involving football player Michael Vick,[1] who was engaged in dog fighting and was prosecuted on related charges. The reaction to Vick's dog fighting was ubiquitous; everyone condemned him. And the reaction to Vick was not just criticism; people were morally outraged by his conduct. Why? The answer is simple: He violated a moral principle that the overwhelming majority of us accept, that we see as representing a moral truth. And given the acceptance of that principle, logic and rationality require that we also see that we cannot distinguish what Vick did from what anyone does who imposes suffering on any animal for no reason other than pleasure, amusement, or convenience. This understanding requires that we be vegan and that we seek to abolish all animal use.

If you see that the first premise is true as it concerns dogs and if you want to act morally with respect to those animals, neither of which are matters of

---

[1] See http://www.truth-out.org/news/item/8459-thinking-about-mitt-romney-and-seamus-michael-vick-and-dog-fighting-and-eating-animals

logic or rationality, then analogical reasoning can be used to demonstrate that there is no morally relevant difference between the dogs you regard as members of the moral community, and all other sentient nonhumans. It's a matter of logic only *after* there is an acceptance that animals, or at least some animals, matter morally. We can use logic and rationality to show that welfare reform and, indeed, anything short of abolition will fail to discharge our obligations to nonhumans given their moral significance.

But if we do not accept that animals have moral significance, then arguments about whether we should use animals, or how we should treat them, whether based on rights theory, utilitarianism, virtue ethics, or anything else, will make no sense.

As I discuss in *Introduction to Animal Rights,* the notion of equal inherent value is not in any way mysterious or metaphysical. It is a logical notion that concerns the minimal requirements for membership in the moral community, and it requires that we accord animals the moral right not to be treated as things. This is another way of saying that it requires that we abolish animal exploitation. But if we do not accept that animals belong in the moral community in the first place, or if we don't care about acting morally, the notion of animals having equal inherent value is not going to be of much use.

We all reject human slavery because we recognize that it places those who are enslaved outside the moral community entirely; it reduces them to things. Given that we accept as a matter of moral intuition that all humans should be included in the moral community, that they should be regarded as moral persons and not things, then whatever else this requires, it requires that we abolish slavery. Similarly, if we see animals as having moral value, then, whatever else that requires, it requires that we abolish their status as property, as things, and that we treat them as moral persons. And this requires that we stop consuming them. Period.

But if we do not see any animals as having moral value—and that is a matter that cannot be "proved" in some "objective" or "scientific" way—then logical arguments about what animals should be regarded as moral persons and what moral personhood requires will be meaningless.

What is the Source of Moral Concern?

What if someone does not accept the first premise? What if someone simply does not see any animals as members of the moral community? Can we prove that they are wrong? No, of course not.

Changing moral behavior requires some affective component. In order to be open to logical analysis of the animal issue, you have to see animals as members of the moral community and have to want to act on that insight. That is not a matter of logic and rationality. You have to *feel* that what Simon the Sadist is doing to the dogs is bad, that what Michael Vick did to his dogs was bad.

A similar way of thinking about moral concern is offered by Professor Gary Steiner, who discusses the concept of kinship with nonhumans in his book, *Animals and the Moral Community: Mental Life, Moral Status, and Kinship.* Steiner argues that we need some concept of kinship, or felt connection between human and nonhumans, as a prelude to serious thinking about animal ethics.

I agree with Steiner in that I think that most of us have a predisposition to a sense of kinship with animals. It needs merely to be awakened; we need to become aware of it. This awareness enables us to see the truth of the first premise. This awareness can be triggered by many things, alone or in combination with others:

It can come from our relationship with a companion animal.

It can come from a perception about the interconnectedness of life, or of some norm such as the "golden rule." This may have a spiritual or non-spiritual dimension.

It can come from embracing the principle of nonviolence as a fundamental moral truth. Again, this may have a spiritual or non-spiritual dimension.

It can come from a religious perspective, such as the one that Francis of Assisi had.

It can come from visiting a slaughterhouse.

It can come from reading literature or poetry.

It can come from some aesthetic experience.

In short, there are many occasions for becoming aware of our moral concern. But whether we call it moral concern or a sense of kinship, it is imperative to understand that this must include a moral impulse to want to follow through and to act in ways that recognize and respect the moral value of animals or that actualizes our kinship with them.

Once we have moral concern or a sense of kinship that includes the moral impulse and want to do the right thing by animals, then it makes sense to talk about using logic and rationality to argue to particular conclusions about the scope of the class of nonhuman persons (in my view, all sentient beings) and what their status as moral beings requires of us (in my view, the abolition of all animal use). Until we have this moral concern and the impulse to want to act in a way that recognizes the moral status of animals, logic and rationality will fall on deaf ears.

Abolitionist Advocacy

If someone accepts the first premise (and please remember that, in this essay, I am only talking about one of the many arguments I make in my work), then we can argue logically and rationally that they should stop eating, wearing, or otherwise consuming all animal products and should go vegan. They should support the abolition, and not the regulation, of animal exploitation.

But when we engage in this sort of educational activity, we are generally not using logic and rational argument to try to convince someone of the truth of the first premise; we are using logic and rational argument to get the person to see that her moral concern about animals, properly understood, requires that she come to certain conclusions (veganism and abolition) rather than to other conclusions ("compassionate" consumption, "happy" animal products, welfare regulation, drawing lines between meat and dairy or between fish and cows, etc.).

Is it possible for someone to say, "I care about animals and I agree with your logical analysis but I like animal products so much that I am not going to stop eating them"? Sure it is. But that sort of situation is generally not one that involves a failure of logic or rational analysis. Rather, the person making such a statement most likely does not really regard animals as having moral significance irrespective of what she says. There is a lack of moral concern.

For example, there are people who fetishize dogs or cats. They do not really think of these animals as members of the moral community. Rather, they have some aesthetic or other possibly obsessional reaction to them that is really no different from the sort of reactions that people may have to cars or clothing or other *things*. We have all encountered eccentric people who are obsessed with dogs and have a house full of them but who eat every other sort of animal and who will not even engage on the matter of animal ethics. Caring about animals in a moral way is not a matter of "liking" them or thinking that they are "cute." It is a matter of moral vision, of seeing animals as beings with moral significance and caring about that insight.

Alternatively, we can say that such people have moral concern but lack moral impulse. In my view, to really have moral concern *is* to have a moral impulse. The best guide to what a person *believes* morally is what she *does*. So although I think that moral concern and moral impulse can be separated for purposes of explanation, I regard moral concern in the absence of moral impulse to really be an absence of moral concern.

There are, of course, situations where someone believes that some animals have moral value but does not accept the analogical argument that all sentient beings are full members of the moral community.

For example, some animal advocates, such as Peter Singer, regard all sentient beings as members of the moral community but regard only those with humanlike cognition and, in particular, a humanlike sense of self-awareness, as full members of the moral community. Singer rejects my argument that all sentient beings are similarly situated in that all sentient beings value their own continued existence even if they do not all think about existence in the same way as normal humans do.

There are also situations in which someone believes that animals have moral value but rejects the argument that abolition is the only rational response to recognizing that animals matter morally.

Virtually the entire animal "movement," as represented by the large new welfarist organizations, disagrees with me about the structural problems with animal welfare reform and the need for an abolitionist vegan baseline. They claim that welfare reform will make matters better for animals now and will lead to good consequences for animals in the future. I disagree.

There are situations in which people claim to regard animals as members of the moral community but also claim that we can apply a framework to analyze our moral obligations to animals that is different from the one we use with respect to humans.

For example, some have argued that we should not talk about moral rights or generally applicable rules and that instead, we should be guided by an "ethic of care" that takes into account all of the particulars of a situation. But these people would never apply an ethic of care to fundamental issues involving humans. For example, no advocate of the ethic of care would argue that the morality of rape was dependent on whether that conduct was undertaken with "care" in a particular situation. Rape is always wrong because it violates a right of bodily integrity. Similarly, where fundamental animal interests are involved, we must use a similar analysis and cannot say that "care" suffices or we ignore an essential aspect of moral analysis: the requirement that we treat similar cases in a similar way.

In all three cases, we need to focus on what logic and rationality tell us given that we all agree that animals matter morally and we want to do what is right; we want to know what our moral obligations are. Logic and rationality are an important part of identifying moral obligations precisely because we regard animals as members of the moral community and we have the moral impulse to do what is right with respect to nonhuman animals.

But the important point for present purposes remains that in all cases the source of that moral concern or moral impulse is irrelevant.

If someone cares about animals as moral beings, it does not matter whether her moral impulse was triggered as the result of her relationship with a companion animal, reading about St. Francis, reading a novel like *Black Beauty* or a poem, such as Byron's *Inscription on the Monument of a Newfoundland Dog,* believing in the principle of nonviolence, or the golden rule, or the interconnectedness of life, or as the result of her aesthetic revulsion to bullying.

What matters is that she has the moral concern and the desire to want to act in accordance with it. What matters is that she sees the moral truth of the first premise at least with respect to some animals. What matters is that she accepts as a moral truth that at least some animals are members of the moral community; that they matter morally. What matters is that she perceives the need to act in accordance with her concern. It is then and only then—when she *wants* to do the right thing with respect to the animals that she thinks matter morally—that we can use logic and rationality to demonstrate that her moral concern should extend to all animals and that it requires that we abolish, and not regulate, animal use. It requires that *she* stop participating in animal exploitation. She may not accept, or accept immediately, the arguments for equality, abolition, and veganism but she really won't even understand them in the absence of a moral concern about animals.

The notion that moral concern or a sense of kinship or whatever you want to call it cannot come about as the result of her religious or spiritual views is as silly as saying that moral concern cannot be awakened as the result of a relationship with a companion animal without any involvement of religion or a spiritual tradition. Religion and spiritual traditions are a problem in this regard only when they limit moral concern and decrease the class of those about whom we care morally; only when they restrict a sense of kinship; only when they encourage violence rather than nonviolence. And let's not pretend that secular frameworks cannot similarly limit moral concern. They can, and they are equally objectionable.

Frankly, I do not care whether a person regards nonhumans as members of the moral community because of their religious or spiritual views or their atheistic views or their agnostic views or any other framework.

I don't care whether the source of someone's moral concern for animals is reading the *Sermon on the Mount* and being inspired to think that Jesus was referring to all beings, or whether the concern and inspiration comes from reading the poetry of Byron, who was an atheist, or, as in my case, visiting a slaughterhouse and coming to understand at a fundamental level that the principle of nonviolence is meaningless if it does not include all sentient beings. It was then that I understood the implications of the moral intuition that suffering is bad; that suffering and death always need to be justified by a compelling reason.

I am not saying that we should use the *source* of our moral concern to *argue* for animal rights. That would make no sense. If the source of someone's moral concern for animals is that she read *Black Beauty* as a child, I am not saying that we should promote reading *Black Beauty* as a means of advocating animal rights. Indeed, there are plenty of people who read *Black Beauty* as children and who did not become vegans. But that book (or any number of countless other books, experiences, etc.) may have triggered the moral impulse in someone that makes her receptive to rational arguments we can make as abolitionists to get her to see all sentient beings as members of the moral community and veganism as the only coherent response given her moral concern. If, however, she has no moral concern in the first place, she will not be receptive to those arguments.

As long as there is moral concern and the moral impulse to want to do the right thing by animals, we *can* use rationality to demonstrate why this moral concern should extend to all animals and why abolition and veganism are the logically appropriate responses to the felt recognition, whatever its source, that animals are members of the moral community.

But in the absence of wanting to do the right thing, it will make no sense to discuss what logic identifies as the right thing to do.

* * * * * *

The World is Vegan! If you want it.
Gary L. Francione
Board of Governors Professor, Rutgers University
©2012 Gary L. Francione

Further Reading

Books

Gary Steiner, *Animals and the Moral Community: Mental Life, Moral Status, and Kinship* (Columbia University Press 2008).

About the Authors

Gary L. Francione is Board of Governors Distinguished Professor of Law and the Nicholas deB. Katzenbach Scholar of Law and Philosophy at Rutgers University School of Law.

Anna Charlton is an attorney and Adjunct Professor of Law at Rutgers University School of Law. She was the co-founder and co-director (with Gary L. Francione) of the Rutgers Animal Rights Law Clinic from 1990-2000.

50984843R00095

Made in the USA
Charleston, SC
09 January 2016